All about the Collie

Also in the 'All about . . .' series

THE BASSET HOUND
THE BEAGLE
THE BEARDED COLLIE
THE BOXER
THE BULL TERRIER
THE CHIHUAHUA
THE COCKER SPANIEL
THE DACHSHUND
GAZEHOUNDS
THE GERMAN SHEPHERD DOG
THE GOLDEN RETRIEVER
THE JACK RUSSELL TERRIER
THE LABRADOR
THE OLD ENGLISH SHEEPDOG
POODLES
THE ST BERNARD
THE SHETLAND SHEEPDOG
THE SPITZ BREEDS
THE YORKSHIRE TERRIER
DOG BREEDING FOR QUALITY AND SOUNDNESS
OBEDIENCE TRAINING FOR DOGS
YOUR DOG'S HEALTH
YOUR PET PUPPY

All about the Collie

ADA L. BISHOP

PELHAM BOOKS

First published in Great Britain by
PELHAM BOOKS LTD
44 Bedford Square, London, W.C.1
APRIL 1971
SECOND IMPRESSION OCTOBER 1975
SECOND EDITION MARCH 1980

ISBN 0 7207 1215 7 2ND EDITION
(0 7207 0450 2 1ST EDITION)

Typeset by Granada Typesetting. Printed in Singapore

Contents

Illustrations

Acknowledgements

The author would like to express sincere thanks to those who have given such willing assistance and advice: Lt Cdr J. S. Williams, the Secretary of the Kennel Club, for permission to re-print the Standards of the Breeds and list of charges; Mr T. Robinson and Mr S. Williams for their explicit line drawings; Mrs S. Robinson for her invaluable assistance.

1 The Rough Collie: Origin

The exact origin of the Collie has always been somewhat vague, although the ancient 'shepherd's dog' is believed to be his ancestor.

There seems to be little doubt that the Collie descended from the ancient shepherd's dog which, it is believed, was introduced into this country by the Romans to guard their sheep.

The Collie is one of the oldest British breeds, and can be traced back to the sixteenth century. As we know, the Collie is believed to owe a great deal to the Scottish shepherds who, in the early days, did so much for the breed both in the development of his looks and most certainly in his temperament. One must realise that a kindly nature is essential to a dog who must work sheep and lambs over a wide area in the Highlands, often out of sight of the shepherd. Consequently a bad tempered dog was not encouraged nor was he kept to breed from.

Describing the dog of the Highlands 150 years ago, Burns wrote:

'His breast was white, his touzie back,
Weel clad wi coat o'glossy black;
His gawsie tail wi upward curl,
Hung owre his hurdies wi a swirl.'

The original name was Colley, which I believe was derived from Col, being the Anglo-Saxon for black; this was, of course, the original colour of the breed.

There have been reports of Setters (Gordon and Irish) and also the Newfoundland being crossed with the Sheepdogs, but we shall never really know if this was so. My own belief is that the Collie was bred by the Highland Shepherds who, by selective breeding, endeavoured to maintain a dog with whom a complete understanding could be established. This, in my opinion, is still one of the most important and endearing characteristics of the breed.

This early dog was not as high on the leg as our present-day Collie. He was much broader in skull and shorter in head and had a much more pronounced 'stop'. Selective breeding produced dogs of stamina, and gradually the breed made headway; so we come to the Show Collie, first exhibited at Birmingham Dog Show in 1860, when a Class was provided for 'Sheepdogs of all Varieties'. It was not until the 1860s that the Collie began to establish itself, and in 1871 Old Mec and Old

Cockie were shown. Old Cockie was second to Old Mec, who was owned by Mr Henshall of Salford; Old Cockie was bred by Mr White of Nottingham. This dog had a very great influence upon the breed.

It is interesting to note that at Birmingham in 1872, one class each for dogs and bitches attracted twenty-eight entries. The class of twenty-four dogs was won by Old Cockie and the other class, of only four bitches, was won by Wolf, the only female considered by the judge to be worthy of a prize. This was really the commencement of the Exhibition Collie. In 1875 the number of exhibits increased considerably, and so began the popularity of the breed.

At this point I feel I must mention another theory of the origin, although I consider it hard to believe. It is a theory based on a reference made by Dr Johannes Caius, physician to Queen Elizabeth I. He refers to a group of dogs, *Canis pastorales,* which could include the breed now known as the Collie, but there is no known description of appearance or origin. Many of the earliest authors mention *Canis pastoralis* or *Canis villartiori,* the former being a farm dog and the latter possibly a watch-dog or town dog.

At the end of the eighteenth and the beginning of the nineteenth century, writers put forward the idea suggested by Harrison in 1585, that Icelandic dogs of the period had been brought to England and that the Collie was a direct descendant of those dogs. This theory can still be heard today, but is in fact incorrect. One such dog was 'Jakkie', who would have been considered a Spitz breed today, and it is thought that the dogs which Harrison referred to must have been Icelandic dogs with heavy ears. (This factor is known to occur in Scandinavian Spitz dogs even today.) This rules out the comparison with the Collie.

In the *History of the Quadrupeds* (1792), Bewick shows a wood engraving of a Collie which could well be one of the ancestors of today's race, whilst *Der Hund in seinen Haupt- und Nebenrassen* (1866), by H. G. Reichenback, illustrates two Icelandic dogs of the same type as Bewick's Collie; this surely proves two distinct breeds.

It is probable that the reason no one devoted much time to the exact origin is that most farm and town dogs throughout Europe were so thin and nondescript that they were not really worth the trouble. The hunting and killing dogs owned by the noblemen were naturally held in greater esteem.

From the time of the earliest settlements, men had sheep, and dogs to herd them. From East to West, Turkey to Ireland, a main type emerged, to be known as the Bronzedog, whose forefathers were the oldest farm and town dogs. Evidence dates back some 8,000 years, so these were the first European Sheepdogs.

This dog was used extensively to work the flocks, but as the flocks became larger and the danger of attack by wolves and bears (and indeed human beings) became greater, it was unable to protect its charges. A Bronzedog/Wolf cross, therefore, was made, and this shepherd dog took on the work. The cross is believed to have spread throughout Europe, and in this country was known as Cur-Dog.

When the progression of time brought the disappearance of the great animals of prey and a consequent decrease in sheep stealing, it was felt that these dogs were too dangerous, savage and expensive to keep, and so a change of temperament was required.

In consequence there was a reversion back to the town and farm dog. This transition from shepherd dog to the offspring of the Bronzedog which with time became commonly known as the sheepdog, took place throughout Western Europe and in particular in England, where the transition to sheepdogs occurred in the 1300 to 1400 period.

There were only a few varieties left of the sheepdog; the Bronzedog/sheepdog leads to the Collies of today.

2 Pillars of the Breed

In a book of this size it would be quite impossible to list the exhibitors and their winning dogs in detail prior to the beginning of this century, and I am sure that to most readers such a list would be rather boring. It is, however, necessary to mention some of the most prominent exhibitors and dogs.

It must be realised that sometimes a dog would appear under different names. For example Old Cockie was also shown under the name Cockie Boy. I have always been told that this dog was the outstanding dog of his day. Trefoil too, was a sire to whom we owe a great deal; he was the sire of Ch. Charlemagne and was owned by Mr S.E. Shirley. Mr Shirley was a prominent figure in the foundation of the Kennel Club, other dogs owned by him being Tricolour and Tartan.

Birmingham still seemed to be the main attraction for shows and in 1876 Meg (sired by Trefoil, ex Lassie) was exhibited by the Charles brothers. Unfortunately, one of the brothers died, but the prefix 'Wellesbourne', under the ownership of Mr William Charles, became famous and Ch. Wellesbourne Conqueror figured in many pedigrees.

It was, I believe, about this time that competition started to become keener, when Reverend Hans Hamilton with his Champion Madge became one of the pillars of the early days. (The name of Revd Hans Hamilton is familiar to most lovers of the Collie, his name being kept in the forefront today by the Revd Hans Hamilton Memorial Trophy, competed for at the Annual Championship Show of the British Collie Club.) This gentleman produced Champions Woodmansterne Tartan, Woodmansterne Piccolo, Woodmansterne Thistle, Woodmansterne Thea and Woodmansterne Ivan, and many others including Champion Christopher.

Champion Christopher was sold to Mr T. Stretch of Ormskirk for £60 and he eventually went to Mr Mitchell Harrison of Philadelphia for £1,000. His sire was Champion Metchley Wonder, for whom Mr Megson (previously a successful exhibitor of Dalmatians, St Bernards and Mastiffs) paid £500. These sums of money were extremely high, taking into consideration the value of money at that time.

The first Collies of note were the Tri-colour Champion Chieftain, Champion Bruce, Champion Rutland and his sire Champion Wolf, Champion Caractacus (who was bought at a show in Liverpool by public auction for £350), Champion Metchley Wonder and his grand-sire Edgbaston Marvel (who did much for the breed). Others included Champion Edgbaston Fox, Champion Donovan II, Champion Southport Pilot, Champion Southport Perfection (purchased for £1,005), Champion Pitch Dark, Champion Southport Sunlight, to name but a few and, of course, Champion Ormskirk Emerald.

Champion Ormskirk Emerald was born on 3 September 1894, bred by Mr W. P. Barnes of Aughton. His sire was Heather Ralph (by Champion Stracathro Ralph ex Apple Blossom), his dam Aughton Bessie (by Edgbaston Marvel ex Wellesbourne Ada). This was a difficult dog to handle and not a big winner in his first year of showing as he did not have a very big coat; later, however, he did reach the highest pinnacle and at the height of his career was sold by Mr Stretch for £1,300 to Mr Megson. It was believed that Edgbaston Marvel was taken in part-exchange. Mr Megson later sold Emerald to the Hon. Mrs Chetwyn who rarely showed and who eventually had to disband the kennel. Emerald went up for sale by auction, but as no bids were received he was eventually bought for £2 and given to Mr Santo, the former kennel manager for Mrs Chetwyn. This is an interesting story, even more so when it is known that Mr Barnes was the brother-in-law of Mr H. Ainscough of the Parbolds; the litter from which Emerald came was bred on the advice of Mr Ainscough, Mr T. Stretch purchasing the whole litter with the full consent of his good friend Mr Ainscough for £25.

The mention of Ormskirk Emerald brings me to Mr T. Stretch and some more of the Ormskirk Champions, Champion Christopher, Champion Rufford Ormond, Champion Ormskirk Olympian, and Champion Ormskirk Foxhall. Possibly the dog who did the most for the breed at this time was Champion Christopher. Before leaving the country he sired many well-known winners, as did his son Edgbaston Marvel, who in turn was the sire of such famous Champions as Southport Perfection, Southport Pilot and Portington Bar None.

Mr J. Powers' Barwells, Mr Packwood's Billesleys, Mr Wildgoose's Canutes, Mr David Pollock's Doons, Mr Wheeler's Edgbastons, the Ormskirks, and Mr H. Ainscough's Parbolds, Messrs. Holm and Holliday's Ruffords, W. E. Mason's Southports, and Mr Charles's Wellesbournes were all, by the year 1892, prominent winners in the Collie Stud Book Show Records.

It may be interesting to know how the Parbolds began, since most of our present day dogs trace back to the Parbolds.

In the late 1870s, Mr Ainscough purchased his first Collie, a tri-colour bitch named Sweet Fanny (by Rob Roy Macgregor ex Sweet Lassie), for whom it is believed he paid £20. She produced her first litter by Champion Metchley Wonder. Being satisfied with this litter,

Sweet Fanny was sent for a return visit, and as a result of this mating the first Parbold Champion was born, Parbold Rover. Shown as a puppy at Birmingham and catalogued for £100 he was claimed by Mr Chance who showed him successfully in the name of Champion Great Alne Douglas.

Champion Parbold Picador (born 6 October 1910). Bred by Mr W. Preston. By Master Willie ex Moss Hill Vera.

In studying the photograph of Champion Parbold Picador, note from the pedigree shown that he was a great grandson of Champion Parbold Piccolo and the great-great grandson of Parbold Pinafore. To both of these Mr Hugo Ainscough attributed much of his success as a breeder. Picador was a wonderful example of the Parbold type which he passed on to so many of his progeny, which included many Champions. Parbold Pinafore was born on 27 April 1898, also bred by Mr Ainscough (by Ch. Balgreggie Hope and Parbold Prim). The photograph taken shows her at four years of age, and shows the type of bitch from whom this excellent stock was produced.

Parbold Pinafore (born 27 April 1898). Bred by Mr Hugo Ainscough. By Ch. Balgreggie Hope ex Parbold Prim.

A second bitch was purchased by Mr Ainscough, by Bonaparte ex Wirral Nell. This bitch was mated to Champion Great Alne Douglas, and two well-known winners resulted from this litter, Champion Barwell Pearl and Parbold Patti. Tabley Rose was another bitch purchased by Mr Ainscough, and she was mated to Edgbaston Marvel. This bitch then produced Champion Southport Pilot, Champion Southport Perfection, and many other well-known winners. The Parbolds were by this time becoming established, and another bitch, Parbold Peri, was mated to Champion Sefton Hero, which mating produced Champion Chorlton Phyllis and Champion Chorlton Priscilla in the same litter.

Pedigree of Champion Parbold Picador (born 6 October 1910). Bred by Mr W. Preston.

Master Willie	Ch. Anfield Model	Ch. Parbold Piccolo Bellfield Beauty	Ch. Wellesbourne Conqueror Parbold Pinafore Ch. Wishaw Clinker Bellfield Buttercup
	Sweet Mary	Parbold Pierrot Rose of Rossendale	Ch. Parbold Piccolo Irthlingboro' Day Dream Rossendale Clinker Ladysmith
Moss Hill Vera	Moss Hill Pathfinder	Parbold Prior Moss Hill Clarice	Ch. Anfield Model Sweet Mary Ch. Parbold Peacock Marjorie of Garthowen
	Moss Hilarity	Parbold Prior Moss Hill Clarice	Ch. Anfield Model Sweet Mary Ch. Parbold Peacock Marjorie of Garthowen

Balgreggie Hope was then purchased. He was born in 1896 and was bred by Mr Wilkie. (Balgreggie Hope's mother had been bred by Mr Ainscough.) He quickly became a Champion, and it is to this dog that Mr Ainscough himself attributed a great deal of his success. He was the sire of Parbold Pinafore, and when mated to Champion Wellesbourne Conqueror produced Champion Parbold Piccolo, who was without doubt *the* sire of his time. His progeny include Champion Parbold Pagoda, Champion Anfield Model, Champion Lancaster Rex, Champion Parbold Patentee, Champion Parbold Purity, and Champion Ormskirk Olympian.

Ch. Anfield Model (aged 11 months). Son of Champion Parbold Piccolo and Bellfield Beauty.

There is a story concerning Champion Parbold Piccolo. In 1904, Mr J. H. Behling brought over to America, for one of the greatest prices paid for a Collie, the great Champion Parbold Piccolo, sire of Champion Anfield Model. He arrived at Milwaukee at noon one day in October, disappeared before night, and was never again located. This was spoken of as the greatest loss ever experienced by the Collie fancy in America.

Ormskirk Galopin bred by Mr R. Tait, was the sire of Champion Heacham Galopin, who in turn sired Wishaw Clinker out of Last Rose. I understand that this dog did invaluable service both as a sire and as an example of what a Collie should be. His principal son was Champion Balgreggie Baronet who claims notice in that he was the sire of that corner-stone of Collie history, Champion Squire of Tytton.

At a lecture, my father, the late W. W. Stansfield, had with him a chart six feet deep by seven feet six inches, on which he had traced the breeding of the most notable males from 1873 to 1926 and tried to connect all the best that have built up the Collie stock of that time. According to these findings, the result of different blendings showed the real corner-stones to be Champion Squire of Tytton, through him Grimsby Squire, then Champion Southport Sample and Seedley Squire on to Seedley Superior. Tonge Admiration, Champion Magnet on to Poplar Perfection; Champion Backwoods Fashion, Champion Thane of Athelney and Champion Seedley Sepia also featured. Another line came through Parbold Piccolo, who produced Champion Anfield Model; then came Master Willie, Parbold Prior, Parbold Picador, and Champion Laund Limit; another line ran through Parbold Pierrot, who sired Parbold Paganni, to Ormskirk Foxhall, sire of Champion Parkside Pro Patria, and on to Champion Seedley Stirling, who was the sire of Mountshannon Silver Cloud, who in turn sired Champion Mountshannan Blue Splendour.

It was evident at the time (1926) that the strains were almost identical in composition, the chief part having been played by Champion Anfield Model; Parbold Prior at one time was responsible for a lot of good results, bitches sired by him figuring largely as dams of the most successful strains.

Champion Squire of Tytton was bred by Mr Tom Horry and born in 1904. He was, according to the old Collie men of that time, a very fine specimen, having wonderful bone and substance and a very good coat of correct texture. The Grimsby prefix of Captain Lewis will always be remembered by the members of the British Collie Club too, we have the Grimsby Champion Southport Sample Trophy for competition at the Annual Championship Show. The owner of the Grimsbys left a legacy to the Club for a prize of ten shillings (50p) to be awarded annually from the legacy to the winner of the trophy. Thus is the name of Captain Lewis imprinted upon the world of Collies.

The Seedley prefix was that of Mr R. H. Lord, and upon his death was retained by the kennel manager, Mr Robert Rudman. Mr Rudman was the breeder of Champion Seedley Sepia and many other Champions. The Southports were owned by Mr W. E. Mason who bred and exported many well-known winners to the U.S.A., where at one time Mr Mason lived and established a well-stocked kennel of first-class Collies. Mr Mason will be remembered by the older Collie fanciers as the man who produced *The Collie Folio*, and who later sold this to my father, who then continued this excellent publication until World War 1 made it necessary to close down. The first Collie of merit to be owned by my father was Master Willie, bred by R. H. Whittaker in 1906 by Champion Anfield Model ex Sweet Mary. Pure

Gem, also bred by 'Bob Harry' (as he was affectionately known) in 1908, was the foundation bitch of the Laund kennel. She was by Seedley Squire ex Lady Temple, who was a sister to Master Willie. The first Laund Champion, Limit, was born on 22 March 1912; he was by Champion Parbold Picador ex Laund Lily.

Champion Laund Limit (born 22 March 1912). Bred by Mr W. W. Stansfield. By Ch. Parbold Picador ex Laund Lily.

Another fancier from whom my father learnt a lot was Ted Bridge of the Harwood prefix, along with Mr Whittaker, Mr Stretch, Mr Lord and Mr Ainscough. I still have all the old photographs of Mr Ainscough's dogs and many of the Ormskirks, these having been given by those wonderful men to my father.

Another great fancier at this time was Mr John Haworth of Farnworth. I shall always remember his gentle manner and the kind way he answered my questions when, as a small child, I started to attend the shows with my father. Some of his Farnworth dogs were Farnworth Floss, Farnworth Fossil, Champion Farnworth Model, Farnworth Folio. There were many more beautiful bitches for which Farnworth was noted.

My thoughts turn at this point to the Eden kennel owned by Mr F. Robson, who exhibited in this prefix many famous champions until his death several years ago. Mr H. Ribbins, the kennel manager, also lived in Carlisle where this famous kennel was established. I would like to mention Champion Eden Extra, Champion Eden Elenora and Champion Eden Elegance as being the forerunners of this kennel.

Mr W. Grimshaw of the Parksides was the owner of Champion Parkside Pro Patria, and is still remembered by his many Collie friends as a past President of the British Collie Club, as is Mr Robson.

The North of England has always been rich in Collie lore, and moving along to the Seedleys, perhaps one of the greatest of these was Champion Seedley Sapphire. Mr W. T. Horry wrote of her when judging at the Kennel Club Show at Crystal Palace in 1908:

'Champion Seedley Sapphire (Champion Parbold Peacock, Sweet Mary) just coming into coat. This grand bitch with a lovely eye and expression, any amount of bone, about the best of her sex we have today. Her ears are small, perhaps too small to attain the orthodox carriage, and she is not quite true on her front. Had it not been for these two minor faults I should have awarded her the 60 guinea trophy as well as the Championship.'

The trophy was awarded to Mason's Champion Southport Sample (Grimsby Squire, Hilda of Moreton).

In addition to the kennels already mentioned, there was the St Helens of Messrs. Woosey and Stronach.

Champion Kettleby Gladys (born 13 August 1908). Bred by Mr J. Landers. By Ch. Southport Sample ex Kettleby Pearl.

Just before his death early in February 1970, I was reminiscing with that most endearing character Mr Arnold Clough about the 'old ones'. St Helens Sensation and Champion St Helens Sapphire rapidly came to mind, along with Champion Magnet (by Tonge Admiration ex Southport Seal) owned by Mr Laidlaw of Bolton and later Mr J. Landers in Lincolnshire. Also mentioned were the lovely Champion Kettleby Gladys and her litter brother Champion Kettleby Marquis, who was exported to the U.S.A. They were bred by Mr John Landers, whose first Collie was said to be of the old working Cheviot Hills strain in the early days of 1875; his first pedigree dog of note was sired by Edgbaston Fox. Mr Landers considered that Gladys was possibly the best that he had bred during his thirty years of Collie breeding.

Mr T. H. Van Hattum was the breeder of that good dog Sonnenburgh Squire, his kennel being known in Holland as well as in Maidenhead where he lived.

One could go on for ever giving names of the famous men who did such a great deal for Collies: Mr T. P. Dalzell of Ireland, and later his son Mr A. P. Dalzell of the Knock prefix; Mr Frank Wildgoose and the famous Canutes; Mr H. Mumford Smith and the de Montforts; Mr A. E. Threlfall of the Leylands (at one time Treasurer of the British Collie Club), and the well-known judge Mr James Russell, Mr Jones's Treffynnons, and Mr Taylor's Kinnersleys.

The 1914–18 War dealt a savage blow to the dog fancy as a whole, but it was not very long after the Armistice that breeding commenced in earnest again, and many new names began to make their presence felt in the awards. Mrs Hume-Robertson was one of the first ladies in the breed. She scored heavily as the breeder of that lovely blue merle Champion Porchester Blue Sol. Miss Daisy Millar too had a measure of success with merles, her Gipsyville Blue Minx being a well-known winner.

Mr R. J. Davies with the Reformers, Mr Bart Hewison's Hewburns, Mr Raynor Anderson's Saltaires, Mr R. H. Roberts's Ashsteads, Mr Cyril Pearce's Eltham Parks, Mr Bennett's Sedgemoores, Mr L. H. Hayter's Athelneys, Mr F. W. Ball's Backwoods, Mr T. Harrison's Freshfields, Mr Allsopp's Merrions and now, of course, Mr R. Rudman had the Seedley prefix. 'Delwood' was the prefix of Col. and Mrs Wilberforce, who had at their home in Fulford a dogs' cemetery and as each of the old favourites died, a little headstone was erected to their memory. It was amongst these headstones that the ashes of their beloved master were scattered one very sad day. This charming couple were devoted to each other and to their dogs. When Mrs Wilberforce passed on, money was left in trust, and there are still a few Collies who bear the Delwood prefix and who live at Delwood Croft.

Mrs James owned the Mariemeau prefix and the Alphingtons were owned by Mr A. E. Newbery. It may be of interest to some to know that Mr J. A. Taylor of the Moss View Collies was the father of the late Mr W. Hindley Taylor. In Scotland, the Watt family kept the Collie flag flying with the Netherkiers and the Dyfesdales and Mr John Shearer will be remembered by the many admirers of Champion Garniehill Pride; his daughter Mrs Margaret McAdam is still interested, and her Helengowan prefix will be familiar to many in both Collies and Shetland Sheepdogs.

The Beulahs were owned by the late Mrs N. K. George and the Westcarrs by the late Miss Clare Molony. Both these ladies were frequently to be seen at the Shows. Mr and Mrs Cliffe owned the Lyncliffes, which were usually handled by Mrs Cliffe. Mr Harold Cliffe died recently, and we do not now see much of Mrs Cliffe.

I have a British Collie Club list of Judges for 1938; it contains the names of thirty people who are sadly no longer with us but to whom we owe so very much that I feel privileged to have known them and the high standard set by them when judging. It is interesting to note that only two ladies were on that list, Mrs H. H. Wilberforce and Mrs R. E. James. The others listed were Col. H. G. Wilberforce, D.S.O., T.D., Messrs W. W. Stansfield, W. Grimshaw, B. J. Hewison, F. W. Ball, A. Clough, F. Robson, A. Dalzell, W. E. Mason, G. Wallwork, H. Ainscough, F. Swan, A. Newton, C. Houlker, T. A. Moffat, R. Anderson, A. E. Newbery, W. Scholfield, J. A. Taylor, T. Butterworth, A. Hyslop, H. E. Packwood, F. Wildgoose, J. Bennet, A. E. Threlfall, W. Birch, J. W. Jones and H. Taylor.

The Collie seems to have been one of the few breeds to be mainly in the hands of the men. Of recent years this has changed and now one sees many ladies in the ring. Unhappily, we no longer see Miss P. M. Grey, whose Ladyparks were so much in the news, Champion Lochinvar of Ladypark being a much used and successful stud dog; he was possibly the best known of the many Champions who emerged from this famous kennel, although some beautiful bitches were born and raised at Ladypark. Miss Grey unfortunately died a few years ago.

Another figure missing from the Collie benches is Mr J. E. Mycroft, whose Mywicks prefix was to achieve fame in the fifties; he was known the world over as the owner of Champion Mywicks Meadow Lancer, and many others including Champion Mywicks Satine of Simbastar, who at the age of nine-and-a-half won her fifteenth certificate in the ownership of Mr D. Rippon, who had become a partner in the Mywicks kennel. On his retirement from business due to ill health, Mr Mycroft, with Mrs Mycroft, decided to visit Australia, leaving the dogs with Mr Rippon. Several judging engagements had been planned, and visits to kennels in Australia and other countries. Alas, this was not to be. The genial President of the British Collie Club was in the ring judging his favourites when he collapsed and although a doctor was on the spot, nothing could be done.

The prefix Mywicks seems in some strange way to be connected with tragedy. Mr Rippon continued to breed and exhibit Mywicks Collies until one sad rainy day in 1978 when Des and Enid left their home in Hackenthorpe to travel to Herefordshire to see a litter of puppies sired by their Blue Merle dog. They were killed in a road accident. They are sadly missed in the world of Collies, especially by members of the British Collie Club Committee, on which they had both served.

This page: Champion Mywicks Meadow Lancer (born 16 March 1955). Bred by Mr J. E. Mycroft. By Mywicks Monitor ex Shoinemaw Sheena.

Centre top: Champion Allison of Shearcliffe (born 3 January 1973). Breeder Mrs A. McCraight. By Shearcliffe Battleaxe ex Coldernice Caprice. Owner Mr J. S. Broderick.

Centre bottom: Champion Danvis Ladyvale Blue Macade (born 26 June 1975). Breeder Mr P. Davison. By Danvis Jefsfire Johnny Walker ex Sea Dreamer. Owner Mr T. D. Purvis.

Far right: Champion Jefsfire Strollaway (born 31 May 1958). Breeders and owners Mr and Mrs A. T. Jeffries. By Ch. Gunner of Glenturret ex Jefsfire Satin Sensation.

Mr Mycroft lived in the Midlands as do many other well-known Collie breeders including that 'Peter Pan' Mr George Archer, who has piloted so many champions to victory, in his Whitelea prefix, Mr Broderick, now domiciled in the Midlands with the Shearcliffes, and we must whilst in this area remember that enthusiastic pair, Mr and Mrs Jeffries, with their Jefsfires. Not far away lives Mrs Franklin, with her Pattinghams, whose Champion Pattingham Pacemaker wrote his name on the Scroll by his wins at Cruft's. Mr Purvis of Danvis fame had a great Best in Show win with Champion Danvis Damascus, and more recently has annexed the British Collie Club Trophy three years in succession with the brothers Champion Danvis Ladyvale Blue Mist and Champion Danvis Ladyvale Blue Macade; the latter also had the honour of being Reserve Best in Show (all breeds) at Manchester.

Mrs Chatfield and her Dunsinanes live in Yorkshire; and most people will have Dazzler of Dunsinane somewhere in the Pedigree of their present day Collie. Although he was not often shown, he was widely used at stud, and was the sire of many well-known winners, one of whom was the well-known Champion Royal Ace of Rokeby and his litter sister Champion Romney of Rokeby. These Rokeby twins were owned by the Eglins in Cheshire, and Ace also went on to sire several Champions. Champion Bririch Gold Edition and his brother Champion Bririch Gold Emblem were two of the early ones owned by Mr and Mrs Hickson. Emblem went to America whilst still quite young; Edition remained at home and in turn has sired his share of winners.

His son, Champion Kidlaine Konrad owned by Mr and Mrs Ainscow of Bolton, has also proved his worth as a sire, one of his sons being Champion Aberthorne Arrester, whose children are at the moment winning Challenge Certificates. It would appear that once again there emerges a prominent male line.

Mr and Mrs Wigglesworth's Champion Sandiacre String of Pearls was the dam of that other well-known stud Sandiacre Softly Softly, who was also sired by Dazzler; it is from this now well-known kennel that many winners have been exhibited and exported.

Far left top: Champion Sandiacre String of Pearls (born 9 September 1967). Breeder Mr C. Chambers. By Ch. Royal Ace of Rokeby ex Seawitch of Sandiacre. Owner Mrs S. M. Wigglesworth.

Far left bottom: Champion Royal Ace of Rokeby (born 20 May 1965). Breeders Mr and Mrs J. Eglin. By Dazzler of Dunsinane ex Ch. Witchcraft of Rokeby.

Centre: Champion Bririch Gold Edition (born 10 June 1969). Breeders and owners Mr and Mrs Hickson. By Ch. Royal Ace of Rokeby ex Ch. Bririch Golden Belita.

This page: Champion Kidlaine Konrad (born 7 May 1972). Breeders and owners Mr and Mrs S. Ainscow. By Ch. Bririch Gold Edition ex Kidlaine Kyano.

Champion Brettonpark Whatzizname bred by Mr and Mrs Duncan, a son of Brettonpark Vanity Fair and Champion Ramsey of Rokeby, has also been much in demand, and many winners own him as their sire.

Mrs Speding and Champion Antoc Vicar of Bray were often seen at the head of a class, and she continues to support the breed.

Top left: Champion Geoffdon Westlynns Wayside Boy (born 11 August 1969). Photograph taken at 9 months. Breeders Mr and Mrs E. J. Westwood. By Ch. Ramsey of Rokeby ex Ch. Westlynns Witchcraft. Owner Mr G. E. Mildon.

Top right: Champion Duntiblae Dogstar (born May 1964). Breeders and owners Mr and Mrs J. R. G. Cochrane. By Ch. Duntiblae Dogwatch ex Duntiblae Dolly Mixture.

Champion Cathanbrae Willow Pattern (born 27 September 1970). Breeder and owner Mrs T. Taylor. By Knightmarksman of Rokeby ex Ch. Cathanbrae Ladypark Lavender Blue.

In the lovely countryside of Shropshire live Mr and Mrs Mildon with the Geoffdon prefix. Both are devoted to the dogs, having a small but select kennel; one can usually see one or two Champions here. Whilst in mid-England there are the Duntiblaes of Mr and Mrs J. R. G. Cochrane. North of the border into Scotland, one thinks of the Narragansettes of Mr and Mrs McLaren, and Champion Snogarth of Narragansette with 5 C.C.s and 8 Reserve C.C.s to his credit.

To mention *all* the well-known kennels of today would require a whole book. The breed has attained such popularity both at home and abroad; often when judging in some foreign country one is told that the dog one has put up has been exported from England by Mrs Taylor and is Cathanbrae-bred, or comes from Corydon and the Blakes, or is in some way related to one of the well-known strains. There are so many kennels that to try to name them *all* individually would be almost impossible; I would certainly offend someone, so I am leaving this undertaking aside. To conclude this chapter, I must say, 'I apologise if I have forgotten or left you out but I am only human and do not have quite the memory of that wonderful animal, the Collie.'

Left: Champion Snogarth of Narragansette (born 14 February 1966). Breeder and owner Mr H. P. McLaren. By Netherkeir Torch Fire ex Jefsfire Satin Symphony.

Right: Champion Corydon Qui Vive (born 19 August 1970). Breeders and owners Mr and Mrs J. Blake. By Corydon Quo Vadis ex Corydon Regality of Rokeby.

3 Blue Merle History

It is to Mr W. P. Arkwright that the Blue Merle really owes its thanks. This gentleman spent many years in trying to breed a Blue Merle, and eventually, using a stud dog of unknown parentage named Scott, he managed to achieve this. Scott was born in 1873 and owned by Mr Brackenburg. Mr Arkwright described Scott as a light silvery blue, beautifully clouded with black; white collar, frill, blaze, paws and tag; face and forelegs bordered by bright red, with one china eye.

Scott was mated to a bitch named Russett, and one of the resultant bitches from this litter was named Blue Stocking. Blue Stocking was later mated to a dog called Redbreast, and Blue Rose was one of the Blue Merle bitches emerging from this litter. A little inbreeding then took place, Blue Rose being mated back to her grandsire, Scott, and in 1882 the much-talked-of Blue Sky and his sister Blue Thistle were born. This was the time when things began to happen, and Blue Sky was said to be the best of his colour and sex of that period; his sister proved herself to become the mother of the celebrated Blue Ruin. Blue Ruin was said to be the best Blue Merle of that period, and a very good ambassador for her colour when she left this country in 1890 to establish the Blue Merle in America. Blue Belle, who again was a daughter of Blue Stocking, was the dam of Blue Bear, who was a winner in 1888.

Mr John Powers also took a hand in the Blue Merle breeding, his Barwell Lass being one of the early names in the award list. Mr F. Barlow and the Yardleys were also prominent: Yardley Blue Jumbo (by Master Merledale ex Yardley Crystal) born 2 July 1906, Yardley Blue Spider (by Master Merledale ex Stoneleigh Lady) born 21 May 1906, and Yardley Freda (by Annandale Knockout ex Annandale Blossom) born 15 October 1906, were some of the early ones.

Mr C. White was also a loyal supporter of the Blue Merle, and his Blue Princess Alice, also born in 1906, was a predominant winner. At Birmingham and District Collie Club on 2 October 1907, Blue Plasmon (by Edgbaston Plasmon ex Hartshill Stella) was the Best Blue Merle, and he was followed by Yardley Merle Nero (by Yardley Black Prince ex Yardley Blue Belle). The Best Female was the puppy Blue Princess Alexandra (by Blue John ex Bonny Girl). Mr W. L. Tippett's Blue Plasmon was only seven and a half months at the time, whilst Mr C. White's Blue Princess Alexandra was only five and a half months.

Also in 1907, Cheetham Hill Show decided to put on a class for Blue Merles, and much disappointment was expressed when it became known that Smooth Merles were to be included in this class; this was considered at that time to be very unfair! The Northern Collie Club was not too happy about its Novice Merle Cup being up for competition when the competition was for both coats, since the Northern Collie Club Trophy was really intended for Rough Merles only. The second prize in the class went to a Smooth; this was reported as being unfair and unsportsmanlike on the part of those responsible for the perpetration of such a fiasco. The situation was relieved when the Cheetham Hill Secretary explained that this mistake was an oversight and the definition of the Blue Merle Class should have read 'For Roughs Only'.

Mr Barlow won the Northern Collie Club Cup for the Best Rough Merle Novice and so had the honour of being the first name to be inscribed on the trophy, his Yardley Merle Nero being the winner. It was also in this year that the inaugural meeting of the Rough Blue Merle Club was held. Mr Fred Barlow occupied the chair and such well known fanciers as Mr C. H. Wheeler, Mr H. E. Packwood, Mr C. White, and Mr T. Leckie were present, whilst many had written to offer their support, including Mr W. E. Mason, Mr T. Horry, Mr J. H. Jacques, Mr T. Baker and Mr A. C. Thompson, Miss Gill-Smith and Mrs Horne.

Mr Barlow was elected President of the Club, Mr T. Leckie the Hon. Treasurer and Mr H. G. Hill, Hon. Secretary, the Committee was made up of the leading Collie men of the time, Messrs T. Horry, J. H. Jacques, W. E. Mason, H. E. Packwood, A. C. Thompson, C. H. Wheeler, C. White and R. J. Warner. The objects of the Club were to encourage the breeding and improvement of the Rough Blue Merle Collie by the holding of shows, and the giving of 'Specials', and endeavouring to induce Show Committees to provide classification for that variety.

A question was also raised with the introduction of the Blue Merle with 'china' or 'wall' eyes. The question was whether or not there was any truth in the theory that the vision of the china or wall-eyed dog was stronger and more powerful than that of others, and also that they would never contract cataract opthalmia or other diseases of the eye. Mr Barlow's Yardley Merle Echo was once the subject of an amusing story: a spectator at one of the shows referred to his wall eye as a 'glass' eye!

Whilst mentioning the Yardleys, Yardley Merle Echo and his brother Yardley Merle Nero were of course, bred by their owner, Mr Barlow. Their pedigree is shown on the following page.

It will be seen that Ashford Royal who was responsible for some of

Yardley Black Prince	Parbold Piccolo	Wellesbourne Conqueror Parbold Pinafore	Wellesbourne Councillor Wellesbourne Beauty Ch. Balgreggie Hope Parbold Prim
	Yardley Crystal	Edgbaston Royal Ellwyn Lenore	Portington Bar None Wilton Dolly Birkie Punch Francesca of Moreton
Yardley Blue Belle	Yardley Blue Emerald	Yardley Merle Rover Yardley Blue Nell	Yardley Merle Emerald Yardley Doonie Yardley Merle Emerald Yardley Doonie
	Yardley Blackie	Yardley Chieftain Yardley Cice	Ashford Royal Yardley Crystal Dudley Rescue Yardley Crystal

Pedigree of Yardley Merle Echo and Yardley Merle Nero.

the earliest winning Smooths, appears in the fourth generation of these typical brothers who were born on 11 July 1906.

Mr Tippett had the distinction of winning the Billesley Bowl with his Blue Plasmon. This trophy was on offer for the first time at Birmingham and District Collie Club. It was considered to be a remarkable feat for a new member to win this trophy with a Blue Merle competing against the Sable and Whites.

Speaking of Birmingham, the oldest of all dog shows (I refer now to the General Dog Show and not to the Birmingham Collie Club), I wonder how many people realise that in the earliest days of the shows held in that city, all the exhibitors were turned out of the building prior to the judges making the awards. The dogs were taken off the benches by attendants and judged in the narrow space between the benches, all award cards then being put up before the owners were again admitted to the hall. The first prize was £10 at that time, so one can imagine the scramble to get back to the benches to find out who had won. It seems unbelievable that dogs could possibly have been judged in these circumstances.

The Northern Collie Club held its fifty-class Collie Show at Derby on 11 January 1908. The turnout of Blue Merles was said to be pleasing. Blue Plasmon won all his classes, whilst Mr H. G. Hill brought out a six-months-old Novice bitch to win all her classes and the Novice Challenge Cup for Best Novice Merle.

The club was now able to announce that two other cups were to be offered, for Best Rough Blue Merle Dog and Best Rough Blue Merle Bitch, confined to members of the Rough Blue Merle Club, such to have been bred by exhibitor; they were to be won three times before becoming the absolute property of the member.

Merles now seemed to be gaining popularity, and it was Mr H. G.

Hill who bred what were in the eyes of many the two best merle bitches. One was Azure Belle, whom he sold for a record price for a female merle and the other was Grey Charmer, said to have a beautiful head. Grey Charmer was out of the bitch Lady of Balsall, who was by Ch. Squire of Tytton; her colour was attributed to her sire, Master Merledale, a celebrated merle sire of that period.

Southport Sky Blue owned by Mr W. E. Mason (by Master Merledale ex Stoneleigh Lady) was born on 21 May 1906, and was a winner of the Merle Classes at Birmingham. He was exported in 1908 to Mr W. Ellery of San Francisco and was Best Merle at New York. In fact the one class provided at this show had drawn twelve entries; this was divided and two sets of prizes were awarded. The first three in the Dog Class were all Southport imports, as also was the winning bitch. Two of these dogs were Southport Blue Boy (by Champion Squire of Tytton ex Southport Blue Cloud) and Greystone Bluebeard, formerly Southport Don (by Master Merledale ex Vaughton Lil). The winning bitch was none other than Azure Belle to whom I referred earlier, now in America and known as Greystone Blue Belle (by Master Merledale ex Rona), owned by Mr Untermyer.

Mr Mason also reported a litter from Champion Southport Sample and Southport Bluey; this breeder, so well known for high-quality sable and whites, was now turning to merles.

Young Merledale (by Master Merledale ex Vaughton Lil), White's Blue John (by Highgate General ex Blue Jennie), Yardley Blue Jumbo (by Master Merledale ex Yardley Crystal), Claypole's Curzon Blue Bubbles (by Curzon Blue Boy ex Curzon Beatrice) and Warley Blue Daisy (by Master Merledale ex Yardley Crystal) were all winning Blue Merles, and helping to popularise the colour. Heads were said, in most cases, to be below the standard of the Sable and Whites.

The Collie Club Show in March 1908 saw Southport Grey Charmer (by Master Merledale ex Lady of Balsall) winning the Merle Classes. Mr Packwood introduced a new dog puppy in Billesley Blue Coat (by Master Willie ex Blue Beauty), and his sister Billesley Blue Belle. The bitches were, at this show, considered to have the better of the dogs. Blue Masterpiece (a brother of Southport Grey Charmer) made his debut and was said to be of beautiful colour. He joined his sister later at the Southport Kennels.

Much activity was taking place in merle breeding, particularly in the Birmingham area, but it seemed that the colour was not always what was required and disappointments were all too frequent. Mr C. White's Handsome Boy was exported to the United States of America, Mr White having bred a litter of five good-coloured merle puppies and one pure white, from Blue John and Strawberry Fair. Mrs Wilkinson was one of the lucky ones too, as she had a litter of five, two tri-colours and three merles, by Yardley Merle Jumbo ex Lassie o'th'Hill.

Southport Blue Flame, in whelp to Champion Southport Sample, was also exported to the United States, this time to Mr E. B. Allen of Massachusetts. Merles were now getting very popular in America, and competition was keener than ever known. In addition it is worthwhile noting that merles were also sent to South Africa.

Mr C. White was delighted to report that his well-known winner Blue Princess Alexandra had whelped three beautifully coloured puppies. This was the thing to be able to announce, really well coloured puppies being born to parents of good colouring, since many of the merles described as such left a great deal to be desired. Blue Princess Alexandra was described by many as 'such a beautiful colour', and from her photographs it would certainly seem that this was so.

At this period the definition of a Blue Merle was not very clear and efforts were being made to agree on a satisfactory definition. It was thought that the 'showily' marked ones would forge ahead. The white collar, legs, tip of tail and blaze gave added attractiveness to the dog of this colour.

Southport Sky Blue, as mentioned earlier, had joined Mr Ellery's Kennel, was much in demand at stud, and was now being placed at stud in various parts of America to enable the breeders to see and to use this much-talked-of dog. The Alstead and Imna Kennels were two of the most prominent kennels to have taken advantage of this service.

Apparently there was at the time a strong contention amongst the men of the Middle West, where large herds of cattle and sheep were raised for the packing centres, that the Collies of this colour were particularly efficient as stock dogs. This was said to be because merles in particular were used for a long time in the sheep pastures in Scotland, and a good dog of this colouring would fetch a handsome price.

Whilst on the subject of the merle as a working sheepdog, I well remember that old Jonathan Holden, a shepherd in the Rossendale Valley where I was born and brought up, frequently used one of father's Blue Merles as a stud dog on his working sheepdogs. As a treat I was taken to see the dogs at work and to see the puppies being trained. It was always the Blue Merles he used as stud dogs, never the Sable-and-Whites or Tri-colours – so perhaps there is some real foundation to this theory.

Mr Tippett's Blue Pietro (by Yardley Merle Echo ex Broughton Beatrice) made his appearance at one of the Birmingham and District Collie Shows and made his presence felt. Mr Thompson's Blue Pilot (by Blue John ex Golden Pippin) was another puppy who was described as being of very good colour whilst the same remarks applied to Hill's Azure Enchantress (by Blue John ex Student Empress). Blue

Yardley Merle Echo	Yardley Black Prince	Ch. Parbold Piccolo Yardley Crystal	Wellesbourne Conqueror Parbold Pinafore Edgbaston Royal Ellwyn Lenore
	Yardley Blue Belle	Yardley Blue Emerald Yardley Blackie	Yardley Merle Rover Yardley Blue Nell Yardley Chieftain Yardley Cice
Broughton Beatrice	Ch. Wishaw Leader	Ormskirk Olympian Hartwood Lady	Ch. Parbold Piccolo Ch. Ormskirk Ideal Ch. Wishaw Clinker Old Hall Duchess
	Broughton Bridesmaid	Ch. Rightaway Broughton Bride	Finsbury Pilot Miss Purdon Ch. Barwell Masterpiece Moreton Lady

Pietro distinguished himself at the show by beating the whole lot, Sables included! Blue Pietro's pedigree is shown above.

The Blue Merle, by the end of 1908, was rapidly gaining ground, and the most successful sires up to date were Master Merledale, Blue John, and Yardley Merle Echo. Better classifications for merles were scheduled, a more thorough understanding of the whole subject of the Blue Merle had been reached, and opinions were being expressed that the Blue Merles were reaching the quality of the Sable and White and the Tri-colours.

This was the time when the aforementioned Mrs Hume-Robertson took an interest in the Blue Merle, having purchased a tri-bitch who was in whelp to Southport Silver King.

It was an established fact that the Rough Blue Merle Club had done valuable work for the Blue Merle. With the increase in popularity and the help of the club, the aggregate for the first year of the club's existence was seventy merles, who competed in the twenty-four classes provided, as against thirty merles competing in eleven classes the previous year. This increase was most encouraging; new breeders were joining the merle cult, and in addition the colour of the dogs was said to be improving generally.

Southport Merletta and Southport Merlena were now to be added to the long list of Southport winners. Merlena o'th'Hill too, was said to deserve her place in the awards, having what was described as a 'more than average' head. Mr C. White had again bred another beautifully coloured dog, Blue General. This dog was a half brother to the lovely Blue Princess Alexandra and was born on 10 February 1908. He was by Blue John ex Fairy Student.

In early 1909, it was reported that more Blue Merles had crossed to America the previous year than the total number of Sable-and-Whites and Tri-colours combined. It was also at the beginning of the same

Pedigree of Blue Pietro (born 22 January 1908). Bred by Miss A. E. Gill-Smith.

year that the Blue Merle Champion was reported in America. She was Valverde Blue Belle who had been imported from England. Later, she was reported as 'almost' having won her title against the other colours – just needing one more point to do so. This was a great boost for the Blue Merles as this bitch would then be the only Blue Merle Champion in the world. In fact, the honour of the first Blue Merle Champion was to go to Champion Leabrook Enchantress.

The merle market was a ready one and the dogs seemed to change hands quite easily. Mr Tippett sold his Blue Pietro to Mr Barlow to make up for the despatch of yet another to America in the form of Yardley Blue Nancetta. (She was a half-sister of Yardley Merle Echo.) Mr Thompson also parted with Blue Pilot to Mr G. Overton, this time a home buyer. The well-known Southport Grey Charmer went to Mrs Lunt in Long Island, and this bitch was mated to Mr Lander's Kettleby Marion prior to sailing.

In spite of all these exports, Mr Walter Birch, judging at Birmingham in January 1909, had a record entry for this colour. There were forty in the five classes provided, and the winner in the dog section was Blue Pietro. The winning bitch at this show was Southport Merletta, and the Novice winner Southport Blue Beard. Many new puppies were exhibited for the first time before Mr Birch at this show.

Much research was being carried out as to the most satisfactory way to breed Blue Merles, and Mr C. White, who had bred merles for about ten years, produced these findings. Bonny Girl, by Champion Wellesbourne Conqueror, did not possess any merle blood. She was mated on four occasions to different merle dogs and her first litter resulted in eleven puppies, five of which were Blue Merles. Out of the second litter of twelve puppies, six Blue Merles were born. The third litter of only three puppies included two blues, one of which became the famous Blue Princess Alice. The fourth and last litter produced two merles out of five puppies. From these litters the number of merles amounted to a total of fifteen out of the thirty-one puppies actually born. Another Sable bitch, Highgate Daisy (who was of merle breeding) was mated to Edgbaston Royal, and she produced three Blue Merles out of five puppies.

The results of six litters produced from one merle dog or bitch, mated to another colour but with merle breeding, gave the following coloured puppies.

1 Five dappled sables and one white puppy out of a litter of six.
2 Three merles who had rather too much white and one all white puppy out of a litter of six.
3 Two merles having too much white resulted from a litter of four.
4 One good coloured merle and one having too much white, out of a litter of five.

5 Two merles and the rest nearly all white, out of a litter of seven.
6 Three merles all too heavily marked with white, out of a litter of six.

It can be seen from these results that the breeding of Blue Merles was not an easy task. There was a great deal of disappointment in the litters being produced, so the ones which were successful really had something to be pleased about. It is no wonder that high prices were paid for the outstandingly good-coloured ones.

There is no doubt that Mr White had the knack of breeding a good coloured merle, and his Blue Ena was no exception to this. She was born on 24 April 1908, by Student Professor ex Blue Princess Alexandra. She even made her presence felt as a puppy when shown at Birmingham.

There was much rejoicing when Queen Alexandra took an interest in the Blue Merle Collie. When visiting the L.K.A. (Ladies Kennel Association) Show, it was reported that Her Majesty saw a brace of Rough Collies exhibited by Mrs Wilkinson, asked what breed they were, and declared them to be beautiful creatures.

Sales were brisk. Merlena o'th'Hill was exported to Monsieur Greeves of France, whilst a young puppy by Blue Jumbo ex Rose o'th'Hill went to Miss Gardiner in Scotland.

Again and again, the same kennels seemed to bring out the chief winners. Mr Tippett produced another good one called Blue Phoebe, and Mr Packwood with Billesley Blue Blossom, but it was Mr Mason who again produced the top winner at the L.K.A. in the home-bred Southport Blue Star (by Master Willie ex Southport Grey Charmer). Blue Star did not remain very long with Mr Mason, as he was purchased by Mrs Hume-Robertson and joined the Porchester kennel to meet Southport Sapho who had already gone there.

It was soon noticed that the Blue Merle classes were becoming better filled than those for other colours at the shows. At Newark, merles averaged eight per class, and several new faces appearing amongst these were Mr Collett's Blue Admiration, Mr Landers's Kettleby King, Miss Bailey's Billesley Blue Betty, and Mr Thorley's Blue de Carlo.

The Blue Merle had now made such an impression throughout the world that Count Volosky from Moscow purchased Southport Blue Beard, and Billesley Blue Coat joined Merlena o'th'Hill in France.

The first merle Champion was reported in October 1909. She was an American Champion, owned by Mr J. H. Anerbach of New York. Mr C. White had bred her and she had been exported by Mr H. G. Hill of Birmingham. Champion Leabrook Enchantress became the world's first Blue Merle Rough Collie Champion. Valverde Blue Belle now owned by Miss Bullocke was still without that one elusive point which would have enabled her to claim the victory then won by Enchantress.

To revert to Mr C. White, it was in 1898 that he first commenced the breeding of Rough Blue Merles. Royal Sapphire, May Bloom and Royal Amethyst were produced in one litter, all becoming winners. Blue Ena, Blue Pandora and Blue Perfection also resulted from one litter. From the same litter that produced the new champion mentioned above, Leabrook Enchantress, came Blue General, also bred by Mr White. Blue Star, Blue Jennie, Blue Leader, Blue Princess Alice, Curzon Blue Boy, Blue Don, Handsome Blue Boy, Blue Princess Alexandra, Blue Major and Blue Jessie were all well-known winners for Mr White, most of them being home-bred.

1910 was the highlight for the Blue Merle fanciers, for this was the year that the Rough Blue Merle Collie Club held its first Annual Show, in conjunction with the Birmingham National in Bingley Hall. Separate classes for Open, Novice and Puppy Dogs, Open, Novice and Puppy Bitches, a mixed-sex class for breeders, and classes for Brace and Team, were scheduled. The club also had its cups and many 'Specials' for competition. Mr A. C. Thompson of Smethwick was elected to judge the Blue Merles, and was said to have eighteen years' experience in this colour. His first bitch was Edgbaston Molly, the dam of Blue Gown by Edgbaston Wonder. Blue Fancy was the mother of Blue Diamond, bred by Mr Wheeler and purchased by Mr Barlow. Mr Thompson was also the breeder of Southport Blue Flame, Blue Jacket and Blue Pilot and also Blue Sapphire. Thirty-six entries were received.

The following year saw an increase in entries; forty-one were received. Mr Packwood did the majority of the winning with his Billesley Blue Bronco, which he had purchased from Mr Fred Barlow. Billesley Blue Bird was the winning bitch, Mr J. Landers with Kettleby Blue Queen following Blue Bird through her classes. Mr Barlow also did some winning with his Blue Pietro and Yardley Blue Sapho.

Mr Packwood seemed at this time to be doing very well, some of the best known Blue Merle winners being Billesley Best Man, Billesley Blue Blossom, Billesley Blue Bonnet, Billesley Blue Bella. Mr Packwood had been interested in Blue Merles for a long time, and he eventually joined the Merle Club in 1911. Up to this point he had held the view that the Blue Merle fancy was not strong enough to run a successful club of its own. However, having seen the progress made by the club, and indeed the general improvement in the Blue Merles, which was possibly due to the fact that classes were put on solely for merles and to the hard work being done by the supporters, Mr Packwood began to take an active part in the club. He was one of the oldest breeders of merles, Billesley Blue being one of the first, her son Yardley Blue Fox bearing the prefix of Mr F. Barlow. Billesley Blue Beauty herself was a winner even against Sable-and-Whites, and the bitch from whom most of the winning Billesleys descended.

Mr Tippett brought out Blue Perseus to do his share and the Wishaw Kennel now had a Blue Merle in Wishaw Blue Lad, a son of Blue Pietro. Mr C. White, who had brought out another winner in Blue Viola, was then taken ill and died. This was a sad blow to the fancy and also to the Club where Mr White was Hon. Treasurer.

As in most things, when one door closes another opens, and Mr Ainscough was another of the old brigade to take up interest in the Blue Merle. The quality of the litter bred by Mrs Hume-Robertson was so high that Mr Ainscough purchased from this litter that beautiful bitch, Parbold Blue Luna. Others from this litter were Porchester Blue Comet, Porchester Blue Vesta and the extremely well known Champion, Porchester Blue Sol. Just how much the blue quality must have

Champion Porchester Blue Sol (born 8 June 1910). Bred by Mrs F. Hume-Robertson. By Southport Blue Star ex Porchester Grania.

improved is shown by the fact that the great Parbolds had taken an active part. Up to now the merles had been behind their colour counterparts in some directions. If the colour had been there, the quality in head had been lacking; alternatively, a lovely coloured body would have a sable head or some other defect. But at last the tide was changing, and both colour and quality were now beginning to combine. This famous litter was born on the 8 June 1910 (by Southport Blue Star ex Porchester Grania). The results from this litter were very good, and a great deal of winning was done. Porchester Blue Sol had a great deal to do with the popularity of the merle, and had a great influence on the breed and to this day pedigrees can be traced back to this very famous dog who at the L.K.A. in 1911 won the Challenge Certificate, defeating all exhibits and colours! Other familiar names for their wins throughout the year were Glengyle Silver, Britisher, Blue Paris, Langham Blue Belle, Glengyle Silver Irish, Blue Bantam, Blue Hyacinth, Frogmore Blue Belle, Blue Charlie Straightaway, Blue Eye o'th'Hill and Farnworth Floss (owned by another stalwart of the breed, Mr John Howarth).

Pedigree of Champion Porchester Blue Sol (born 8 June 1910). Bred by Mrs F. Hume-Robertson.

Southport Blue Star	Master Willie	Ch. Anfield Model Sweet Mary	Ch. Parbold Piccolo Bellfield Beauty Parbold Pierrot Rose of Rossendale
	Southport Grey Charmer	Master Merledale Lady of Balsall	Blue Clink Bonnie Queen Mac Ch. Squire of Tytton Elmcote Model
Porchester Grania	Ormskirk Sample	Ch. Southport Sample Countess of Overdale	Grimsby Squire Hilda of Moreton Ch. Squire of Tytton Overdale Countess
	Ormskirk Dearest	Ch. Squire of Tytton Ormskirk Sweet One	Ch. Balgreggie Baronet Helle of Boston Ch. Parbold Piccolo Parbold Ping Pong

It may be interesting for students of Blue Merle history to examine the pedigree of Porchester Blue Sol. He was the first Blue Merle Champion dog in this country, and marked the turning point for this colour, having proved that a really good merle was worthy of a title. Not only was he a beautiful dog but he was also a sire of many good ones. Mr R. H. Lord's Seedley Blue Boy and Mr A. C. Thompson's King of the Blues were two of these.(Another Sable addict, Mr Lord, had now become Blue Merle minded.)

Miss Daisy Millar and her Gypsyville Blue Minx maintained the high quality which later was upheld by the Revd Salter and his Mountshannons, in particular Mountshannon Silver Cloud and the beautiful Mountshannon Blue Splendour.

One or two Blue Merles were housed at Laund, including Champion Cloud, Champion Laund Laurent, Champion Laund Luetta and Champion Laund Laguna.

It was now generally accepted that the Blue Merle could hold his own along with the other colours and therefore, it is not necessary for me to itemise the many individuals.

Mrs George and the Beulahs must now be one of the oldest established Blue Merle Kennels, having carved a name for themselves prior to World War II. Miss Molony too always had a soft spot for the Blue Merle. Many will remember the lovely Champion Westcarrs Blue Minoru. One always associates Miss Clare Molony and Miss Margaret Osborne who also is a keen supporter of merles. Mr and Mrs Cliffe also, at one time, favoured the Blue Merle, and we remember with nostalgia Champion Lyncliffe Blue Lady. From time to time Mrs Chatfield can be seen showing a Blue Merle and, of course, there is George Archer who is always on the look out for a good merle. More recently we come to Mrs Sargeant and her now-famous Carramars, whose Champion Carramar Boy Blue is perhaps the best from this Kennel.

Mrs Combe is also inclined to favour Blue Merles and Tri-colours and is the owner of the Tilehouse prefix.

Due to the care and thought given by the skilful breeders of the past and present to attain the quality in this colour, which has now reached an extremely high standard, I do not think there will be again any question of the blues being of inferior quality.

Many people prefer a good Merle Blue, whilst others prefer a Tri-colour or a Sable-and-White; I personally, have no preferences regarding the colour so long as the quality is there and the colour complies with the required Standard.

4 Tri-Colours and Whites

Queen Victoria was devoted to her Collies, and at Cruft's Show in February 1891, exhibits from the Royal Kennels included Collies, which won several prizes. Gipsy was said to have been a favourite of Her Majesty and was buried in the Home Park at Windsor on 15 March 1868. Later, some of the prize-winners included Oswald (a Tri-colour by Bachelor ex Ch. Peggie II) and Glen, described as black and tan. There was also Darnley II and the white dog Squire. Darnley, also a prize-winner, was a present to Her Majesty by his breeder, the Revd Hans Hamilton (by Charlemagne ex Ch. Peggie II) and was half-brother to Oswald.

As most people know, Queen Victoria had helped to popularise the Collie, but I wonder how many people realize that some of the Collies which were owned by Her Majesty were white ones. Mr John Storey at the time specialised in White Collies and would purchase any White Collie he heard of in his desire to own the pure White Collie. The first pure white Collie was White Slave bred by Mr Storey (by Snow ex Scotland's Lily); Snowstorm was also white with sable head and patches on body and tail, and Snow was white with a black patch on his face. The Earl of Haddington, it was said, purchased one of these dogs from Mr Storey and presented it to Her Majesty.

White Collies are not shown in this country, but there are a few in other parts of the world. For many years Father McGinley, in America, retained a great interest, but I do not think that since his death this has been sustained.

When judging in Holland in 1968, my co-judge Miss May Young had the opportunity to judge the only white entry; she was judging the dogs whilst I judged the bitches. I was not able to examine this dog, who had a black patched head, but he did not impress me at all. From the view I had of him and apart from his colour, he appeared to be a poor specimen of this breed. I think that the general standard of the White Collie is usually lower than that of the more acceptable colours; this could be one of the reasons why this colour never became popular with breeders and why it is no longer acceptable in this country.

Many people write about Sable-and-White Collies and also about Blue Merles but very few people write very much about the Tri-colour, without whom the colour of both the previously mentioned would be in a sad predicament. I cannot understand why the Tri-colour is not more popular, since I consider that a really 'black' Tri-colour with a rich tan marking and of course, white mane and frill, is a truly magnificent creature, and can hold his own with the best of the other colours any time. We do not have many supporters of this colour. I wonder if this can be because Lassie, the famous film-star Collie, was a Sable-and-White, and the majority of people who buy a Collie as a pet have this in mind when buying their dog.

If this is so, and breeders are breeding with this thought foremost in their minds, I am afraid that soon we shall have some extremely poor colours amongst the Sable-and-Whites.

Tri-colours do not so often find their way into homes as pets, and so those retained by breeders are usually of high quality. During the past year or so we seem to have had a few Champions of this colour. One dog who had a lovely head and expression, who became a Champion a few years ago, was Mrs Tweddle's Champion Andrew of Arcot. The two Challenge Certificate winners at Cruft's in 1970 were also Tri-colours, Mr L. J. Caseley's Champion Thistleblue Bluelands Boy, and Mr C. R. Chambers' Champion Colrenes Mywicks Merlow Moonbeam. Another Tri-colour champion winning his certificates was Laund Luscombe.

His grandmother, owned by Mr and Mrs J. Eglin, Champion Witchcraft of Rokeby, also a Tri-colour completed her title at the Yorkshire Collie Club Championship Show in 1969. Also gaining full championship status with her Tri-colour bitch at Manchester in 1970 was Mrs Chatfield with Champion Shearcliffe Black Belle of Dunsinane – quite a feat for Tri-colours!

Left: Champion Alexander of Arcot (born 9 November 1958). Breeder Mrs M. J. Tweddle. By Ch. Danvis Drifter ex Ch. Antanette of Arcot. Owner Comm. Umberto Corsiglia.

Right: Champion Laund Livia (born 13 July 1965). Breeder and owner Mrs A. L. Bishop. By Ch. Duke of Yeldust ex Laund Lesley.

5   The Standard

The Standard for the breed (Rough) was revised and approved in its present form by the Kennel Club in February 1969. Permission has been granted by the Kennel Club for this to be printed below, for which privilege, my thanks. (The Smooth Collie Standard is given in the chapter on that Variety, page 99.)

This Standard of the Collie (Rough) was discussed very widely amongst the Breed Clubs, and within the Breed Council, which is made up of two delegates from each of the fourteen Breed Clubs under the Chairmanship of Miss C. Molony, who represented the Breed on the Kennel Club Liaison Council. Mr A. Jeffries, the Secretary of the Breed Council, when agreement had been reached after many months of discussion, then sent the Standard to the Kennel Club, who finally accepted it in its present form.

Following the death of Miss Molony, Mr R. Cockcroft became the Chairman of the Breed Council, and after the resignation of Mr Jeffries, Mr J. S. Brodrick took on the duties as Secretary of the Breed Council. He now represents the breed on the Kennel Club Liaison Council.

The aim of all Collie breeders and exhibitors should be to breed or own a Collie which comes as close to the Standard as possible. I have seen as many Collies as most people and in my time many, many Champions, but I have never yet seen the perfect Collie; there is always some slight fault or defect to be found somewhere.

Some years ago, judging was done on a points basis, points being given for certain parts of the anatomy. This practice is no longer carried out, but judges base their judgement on various virtues and faults as laid down in the official Standard of the breed, and must carry in their mind's eye a picture of their interpretations of this Standard, and must not allow their judgement to become swayed by any personal preferences. The only way that one can honestly judge dogs is by having an absolutely unbiased mind and a complete knowledge and understanding of the Standard of the breed as laid down by the Kennel Club.

The Collie Club's scale of points used to be as follows:

Head and Expression	15
Ears	10
Neck and Shoulders	10
Legs and Feet	15
Hind-quarters	10
Back and Loins	10
Brush (tail)	5
Coat and Frill	20
Size	5
	100

The Standard of the Collie (Rough)

Characteristics. To enable the Collie to fulfil a natural bent for sheepdog work, its physical structure should be on the lines of strength and activity, free from cloddiness, and without any trace of coarseness. Expression, one of the most important points in considering relative values, is obtained by the perfect balance and combination of skull and foreface; size, shape, colour and placement of eye, correct position and carriage of ears.

FIGURE 1: Outline showing correct shoulder placement and lovely mane and frill.

General appearance. The Collie should instantly appeal as a dog of great beauty, standing with impassive dignity, with no part out of proportion to the whole.

Head and Skull. The head properties are of great importance and must be considered in proportion to the size of the dog. When viewed from the front or the side, the head bears a general resemblance to a well-blunted, clean wedge, being smooth in outline. The skull should be flat. The sides should taper gradually and smoothly from the ears to the end of the black nose, without prominent cheek bones or pinched muzzle. Viewed in profile the top of the skull and the top of the muzzle lie in two parallel, straight lines of equal length, divided by a slight, but perceptible 'stop' or break. A mid-point between the inside corner of the eyes (which is the centre of a correctly placed 'stop') is the centre of balance in length of head. The end of the smooth, well-rounded muzzle is blunt, but not square. The underjaw is strong, clean-cut, and the depth of the skull from the brow to the underpart of the jaw, must never be excessive (deep through). Whatever the colour of the dog, the nose must be black.

FIGURE 2: Receding Skull.
FIGURE 3: Correct Skull.

Eyes. These are a very important feature and give a sweet expression to the dog. They should be of medium size, set somewhat obliquely, of almond shape and of dark brown colour, except in the case of Blue Merles when the eyes are frequently (one or both, or part of one or both), blue or blue flecked. Expression full of intelligence, with a quick, alert look when listening.

Ears. These should be small and not too close together on top of the skull, not too much to the side of the head. When in repose they should be carried thrown back, but when on the alert brought forward and carried semi-erect, that is, with approximately two-thirds of the ear standing erect, the top third tipping forward naturally, below the horizontal.

FIGURE 4: Pricked
ears and round eye.
FIGURE 5: Low set
ears and mean eye.
FIGURE 6: Correct
ears and eye.

Mouth. The teeth should be of good size, with the lower incisors fitting closely behind the upper incisors, a very slight space not to be regarded as a serious fault.

Neck. The neck should be muscular, powerful, of fair length and well arched.

Forequarters. The shoulders should be sloped and well-angulated. The forelegs should be straight and muscular, neither in nor out at elbows, with a moderate amount of bone.

Body. The body should be a trifle long compared to the height, back firm with a slight rise over the loins; ribs well-sprung, chest deep and fairly broad behind the shoulders.

Hind-quarters. The hind legs should be muscular at the thighs, clean and sinewy below, with well bent stifles. Hocks well let-down and powerful.

FIGURE 7: Straight
stifle.
FIGURE 8: Correct
turn of stifle.

FIGURE 9: Correct
hind-quarters.

Feet. These should be oval in shape with soles well padded, toes arched and close together. The hind feet slightly less arched.

Gait. Movement is a distinct characteristic of this breed. A sound dog is never out at elbow, yet it moves with its front feet comparatively close together. Plaiting, crossing or rolling are highly undesirable. The hind legs, from the hock joint to the ground, when viewed from the rear, should be parallel. The hind legs should be powerful and full of drive. Viewed from the side the action is smooth. A reasonably long stride is desirable, and this should be light and appear quite effortless.

Tail. The tail should be long with the bone reaching at least to the hock joint. To be carried low when the dog is quiet, but with a slight upward swirl at the tip. It may be carried gaily when the dog is excited, but not over the back.

Coat. The coat should fit the outline of the dog and be very dense. The outer coat straight and harsh to the touch, the undercoat soft, furry and very close, so close as to almost hide the skin. The mane and frill should be very abundant; the mask or face, smooth, also the ears at the tips, but they should carry more hair towards the base; the fore-legs well feathered, the hind legs above the hocks profusely so, but smooth below. Hair on the tail very profuse.

Colour. The three recognised colours are sable-and-white, tri-colour and blue merle.

Sable. Any shade from light gold to rich mahogany or shaded sable. Light straw or cream colour is highly undesirable.

Tri-colour. Predominantly black with rich tan markings about the legs and head. A rusty tinge in the top coat is highly undesirable.

Blue Merle. Predominantly clear, silvery blue, splashed and marbled with black. Rich tan markings to be preferred, but their absence should not be counted as a fault. Large black markings, slate colour, or a rusty tinge either of the top or undercoat are highly undesirable.

White Markings. All the above may carry the typical white Collie markings to a greater or lesser degree. The following markings are favourable: white collar, full or part; white shirt, legs and feet; white tail tip. A blaze may be carried on muzzle or skull or both.

Weight and size. dogs: 22–24 in. at shoulder; bitches: 20–22 in. Dogs: 45–65 lb; bitches: 40–55 lb.

Faults. Length of head apparently out of proportion to body; receding skull or unbalanced head to be strongly condemned. Weak, snipey muzzle; domed skull; high peaked occiput, prominent cheek bones; dish-faced or Roman-nosed; under-shot or over-shot mouth; missing teeth; round or light-coloured and glassy or staring eyes are highly objectionable. Body flat sided, short or cobby; straight shoulder or stifle; out at elbow; crooked fore-arms; cow-hocks or straight hocks, large, open or hare feet; feet turned in or out; long, weak pasterns; tail short, kinked or twisted to one side or carried over the back; a soft, silky or wavy coat or insufficient undercoat; prick ears, low-set ears; nervousness.

Note: Male animals should have two apparently normal testicles fully descended into the scrotum.

To me this gives a picture of a beautiful dog with a strong frame, deep shoulders, well coupled body, lithe and active with a handsome frill and feathering. His outlook a combination of grace, strength and affection making him one of the most handsome of the canine race.

It should be noted that in this country predominantly white Collies are not accepted although one does occasionally see white Collies on the continent. In America this was, however, quite a popular colour at one time. My own opinion is that this colour Collie is not nearly as attractive as the colours which are set out in the Standard.

6 Kennel Management and Foundation Stock

I think the most important factor in the management of any kennel, whether large or small, is cleanliness. By this I do not mean just a clean dog, but clean kennels, clean exercising runs, clean feeding utensils, clean bedding and at least once per day, clean water. These factors usually add up to a clean and pleasant kennel and not one which after a visit, a bath and a change of clothes are all one desires! Yes, there are kennels like that. It does not take long to acquire this unpleasant state if one allows the dogs to 'take over' and then becomes overstocked with too many dogs and not enough housing or sufficient help to run the kennel efficiently.

The first thing to consider is space and whether or not you have enough ground for housing and exercising the number of dogs you wish to keep. It is advisable to set and keep to a limit, and not exceed this number of dogs; overcrowding is just as bad in a kennel as in a home, and unhealthy dogs will result from these conditions.

If you aim to keep a fairly large kennel perhaps the following description will appeal to you. This description is of an actual kennel which has been proved to be a successful unit.

The main kennel building built in brick was composed of kennels arranged in a similar manner to the benching at shows (back to back thus preventing the dogs facing each other and consequently barking). The entrance to the main kennel was through the cleaning room and this room was complete with a grooming table containing drawers for keeping brushes, combs, and other grooming tools; cupboards for collars, leads, bench chains, dog coats, etc., and a hand basin with water laid on.

On passing through this room, one entered the main kennel which had large windows for adequate ventilation and central heating was installed for use in the very cold weather. At the opposite end to the grooming room, a door led out to a completely fenced orchard in which the dogs could be exercised; in the event of hot weather, shade was provided by the trees. All the buildings were fitted with electricity as was the adjoining cookhouse and toilet. Opposite the main building were two covered runs for use in bad weather. A separate wooden kennel was available to house six dogs, and this was used for visiting bitches; this kennel also had its own run. The whelping kennels and puppy runs were right away from the main buildings and this prevented risk of infection since the main buildings housed dogs who were regularly attending shows. An isolation kennel was in a completely different part of the grounds.

This is, I think, very near the ideal large-scale kennel, as each dog is housed separately, apart from the litters. In addition, visitors to the kennels did not need to enter the house unless it was required, as all facilities were present at the kennels. Of course this layout occupied about four acres, and it must be appreciated that this was purely a kennel of show dogs and was not a boarding kennel.

If, however, you have not the space for a large kennel such as this, (and nowadays not many of us have either the space or the money to acquire and maintain this kind of venture), you can, with a little care and thought, equip a small kennel in as satisfactory a manner.

Collies should have as much room in their separate kennels as possible. I do not like to see a dog in cramped quarters. Many people I know, house a dog and bitch together; this is not a practice that I follow since I feel it usually leads to trouble. Perhaps this will cause the dog to fret when the bitch has to be taken away or cause dogs to fight about one particular bitch. However, I do not mind young puppies being housed together, as they often play like small children, then rest and fall asleep, and are often less trouble than a single puppy on his own.

Whatever the size of the kennel, it is essential to have a quiet spot for the whelping kennel, as the nursing mother usually dislikes interference from other members of the kennel, and in the early days her comfort is of the utmost importance.

Having provided a kennel, make sure that it has a bed which the dog can sleep on. This should be raised from the floor so that it is out of draughts in the cold winter weather. Many owners provide either wood wool or straw on the bed; another idea is a wooden frame over which hopsack or some other strong material can be fastened; this can easily be replaced as it wears out. Sawdust on the floor of the kennels helps to keep the dogs clean and dry and can easily be changed. It is, however, essential that the floors should be scrubbed from time to time.

As much room as possible should be allowed for your dog to exercise. A Collie is a working dog and must be able to stand and move on good legs and feet; this he will not do properly if he does not have the opportunity. It is vital that sufficient shade is provided for your dog in the summer in order that he may take shelter on hot days. Another point to remember during the warm summer days is to avoid taking your dog for long walks during the heat of the day; it is far better to wait until the cool of the evening.

Regular meal times should count as one of the prime necessities of good management. It is bad to feed dogs at irregular intervals, since the dog becomes used to having his meals at a particular time each day. These times can be arranged to fit in with your own schedule for the day as long as the times are regular. This applies to the one-dog owner just as much as to the owner of a large kennel.

I think that very often the question of stock arises before the thoughts of a kennel, as so often one hears of a Collie which was bought as a pet, eventually becoming the forerunner or even the foundation of a kennel. I cannot stress too strongly that if you intend to purchase your first Collie and you have any thoughts, if it is a female, that you may have a litter from her one day, please buy her from a reputable kennel and not from a dealer. Make careful enquiries before buying any dog from a dealer; a few of them are concerned only to sell dogs and puppies and not with the quality of what they breed. They are not really interested in you or the purchase you have made from them and you could be charged a high price for an indifferent specimen. We have all heard the sad tale of disappointed owners who have learnt the hard way. Good dogs can be bought in these circumstances, but it is as well to take care.

The most satisfactory way to purchase your Collie is to attend one or two shows, if possible Championship Shows or Breed Shows, which may be held in your area. At these shows you will see a large number of Collies and can meet and talk to the exhibitors and breeders, most of whom will be only too willing to answer your questions and advise you regarding the purchase of your Collie. Most of the leading kennels will give you the benefit of the experience gained throughout the years, and if you state your requirements will, if they cannot supply you themselves, put you in touch with someone who has just the dog for you. It should be remembered that these breeders are usually breeding from high quality specimens which in turn can be expected to produce good stock and are not being produced to supply a pet market. These good Collies make pets which are just as delightful in this respect as their less handsome friends.

If you intend to purchase a female as a prospective brood bitch, my advice is to buy the best you can afford from the kennel of your choice. If this is to be a puppy, study very carefully the Standard of the Breed before you even select a kennel; go to one whom you consider has the type of dogs which you admire and come close to the Standard in your estimation. It must be remembered that a large number of breeders will want to retain the best for themselves, but may not wish to keep the entire litter and will be willing to sell you a promising female puppy at a reasonable price.

If you have in mind an older bitch who has already been shown and done some winning, you must realise that this will cost you a lot more money. You will have the advantage, however, of starting with the finished product, and will not have to wait to see how the puppy turns out. This can often be a very wise move and pay dividends, since rearing a puppy is quite an expensive project and sometimes one can be disappointed in the finished article.

I have no doubt that some of you will wish to own a male; again, I say, 'Take advice from someone who has experience of the breed and do not choose a puppy just because he is the first to greet you.' I agree that a good temperament is essential, but there is so much more to go with this.

If it is at all possible, try and see the parents of the puppy and check their temperament, making sure that they are sound healthy animals, but if it is only possible to see the mother of the puppy and she meets with your approval, do not worry unduly if you do not have the opportunity of meeting the father.

If it is your first Collie, choose a strong healthy puppy of either sex, making sure that he or she has good strong bone, a solid well-covered body (I do not mean fat) and evidence of a good coat. Make sure that the eyes are of almond shape and not round. Ears at the age of 8 to 10 weeks can be anywhere; I would not lay too much stress upon them at this age, as they will change from day to day as the puppy grows. Correct placement of shoulder, however, is desirable, as this will not alter as the puppy develops.

It is wonderful to select a puppy from a litter and watch it grow and develop; this to me is a most interesting part of breeding.

We will now assume that having selected your first Collie with the utmost care, you now have a notion to breed and rear a litter of Collie puppies yourself. This you will never regret, I cannot think of any sight more lovely than a 'nest' of Collie babies. Do not imagine this will be terribly easy and all profit; this is not the case. However, the immense pleasure you will get from this venture will outweigh all the hard work and worry entailed.

Having selected the foundation of your kennel – and I cannot stress too strongly the benefit of having one or two really first-class bitches instead of perhaps half a dozen of medium and poor quality – you must now begin to look for a suitable sire for this litter. I would like to emphasise that the strength of any kennel lies in the female line.

The value of a really good brood bitch is something which cannot be estimated in the terms of money. She is without doubt the most valuable commodity in any kennel and these treasures are not easily found.

A really good bitch will produce first-class stock from whatever dog she is mated to, and it is often wise to keep to a particular stud dog if a full litter of top-class puppies has evolved from that mating before.

I have a theory, which I learnt from my father, that the bitch counts as seventy-five per cent in any breeding programme.

It is unwise to breed from nervous bitches, as so often this characteristic will be repeated in the puppies. Once established in any strain, nervousness is not easy to get rid of and may come out in future generations. I am personally as keen on good temperament as I am on true Collie type. A brood bitch with a good harsh coat and well-placed eye, a small pair of ears well carried, of good conformation, with the correct type of head, and above all true Collie temperament, makes her such a delight to own. An added pleasure is to watch such a bitch, as she brings into the world, without any fuss or bother, her puppies, and rears them with such obvious pleasure and affection.

A wise precaution is to worm the brood bitch before mating but remember not to treat her for worms within three weeks of whelping or three weeks after.

7 Breeding

Bakewell's Ten Rules of Breeding should be carefully considered when breeding Collies, and whilst there may be certain questionable details, there is also a lot of sound common sense. I quote these rules for you to study.

Bakewell's Ten Rules of Breeding
1. Correct training of the eye and judgement in the anatomy and physiology of the animal.
2. The correlation of the parts, one to the other.
3. The selection and mating of animals with a view to the fullest development of the most valuable parts, according to the use intended.
4. Select with a view to the perpetuation of essential qualities, to induce form, symmetry, high feeding qualities and great vigour of constitution.
5. Feeding with a view to early maturity for giving development in the least possible time.
6. Shelter and warmth indispensable to perfect development.
7. Variety of food is essential, and this according to the age of the animal.
8. A strain of blood once established, never go outside it for a new infusion.
9. The most perfect care and regularity in all matters pertaining to feeding and kennel management.
10. Kindness and careful training are absolutely necessary.

The one factor which seems to be overlooked by many breeders today is that of colour. Many people are so keen to breed only the Sable-and-White that they fail to introduce any Tri-colour into their strain. The result is that over the years the colour becomes pale, and a washed-out straw shade will emerge. To maintain a good rich Sable, the introduction of Tri-colour is essential. I fail to see why the Tri-colour does not enjoy the popularity of his Sable-and-White brother, since I consider a really good black with a rich tan marking and a dazzling white can give a most beautiful picture standing in the show ring alongside Sable-and-Whites. If one breeds Tri-colour to Tri-colour, it is to be expected that the resultant litter will all be Tri-colour. Tri-colour-bred sable to sable-bred sable can produce either colour, as also can sable to sable with tri-colour grandparents on one or both sides, but the sable from these parents is usually of good tone.

One thing to avoid is introducing any Blue Merle into the Sable-and-White. The colour of both will suffer. I have seen a beautiful Sable-and-White bitch, who was sable-bred for three generations, with a lovely merle eye. One was brown, the other blue, and she had a white fleck in her coat; she had obviously thrown back to the fourth generation which contained quite a high percentage of Blue Merle.

It is essential to use blue-bred Tri-colour to Blue Merles, otherwise the colour of the Merles will suffer, and an almost white will result in the constant breeding of Merle to Merle with, of course, the resultant lack of pigmentation. It will thus be seen that the Tri-colour either blue- or sable-bred, is an essential in the matter of colour. It is thus not difficult to see why we have very few kennels who specialise only in the breeding of the Blue Merle. Some of the earliest kennels to do this were Mrs Hume-Robertson's, whose Porchester Blue Sol is shown; Mr Barlow's Yardley Blue Pietro being a beautiful specimen; and the Billesleys of Mr Packwood.

CHOICE OF THE STUD DOG

Choosing a stud dog is a task which must be given very serious consideration. Please do not use the dog 'down the road' just because he happens to be a Collie. If his bloodlines suit the pedigree of your bitch and if he does not possess the same faults as your bitch, this *may* be all right, but it is wiser to use a dog to try to improve upon your own Collie. For example do not breed from two animals with large round eyes or prick ears or weak hind-quarters. If your bitch has prick ears, try to correct this fault by using a dog with good ears. If the eyes are not well placed or of the wrong shape or colour, try to find a dog with the correct oblique almond shaped eye. (The above faults are, I believe, two of the most difficult to eradicate if once brought into a strain.)

I do not consider that the novice should contemplate in-breeding. It is far too complicated, and it must be remembered that whilst in-breeding may increase the virtues of the respective pair, the same thing happens to the faults, quite often with disastrous results. It can happen that the health of the progeny may suffer. Please do not think I am against in-breeding entirely, but I think this is something which requires a great deal of knowledge and experience and is definitely not for the inexperienced.

Line breeding can be much more worthwhile, and is not nearly as complicated.

Never breed from any animals which you know are not one hundred per cent fit. This can only lead to trouble and large vets' bills.

MATING

Having selected a suitable stud dog, the next step is to inform the owner of the dog that you wish to use him for your bitch and if you can give some idea when you expect her in season, this will be appreciated. You should again contact the owner of the stud dog when your bitch's season actually commences. Usually the time of mating should be between the tenth and fourteenth day of the season when the colour of the discharge has changed from the initial red to a pink shade. There is, however, no hard and fast rule about this. I have known bitches who have been mated earlier than ten days from the commencement of the season to have litters, and I had one bitch who was mated twenty-one days after commencement and produced ten strong healthy puppies. This is, of course, exceptionally unusual. You will find that when the deep-coloured discharge has gone, the bitch will show some interest towards the dog and this is the correct time for her to be mated. Do not wait too long before you take her to be mated. Most stud dog owners would prefer you to go early rather than too late and will often be prepared to keep the bitch for you until the mating has been effected.

I do not propose to go into detail about the actual mating, as a stud dog usually knows just what he has to do and deals easily and efficiently with this. You may be asked by his owner to hold your bitch's head in order that she does not snap at the dog. Please obey this instruction without question as many a young dog has been spoilt by being snapped at by a visiting bitch.

STUD FEES

The stud fee should be paid at the time of the mating unless you have made some arrangement with the owner of the dog regarding the expected litter. You will then be given a copy of the stud dog's pedigree.

The fee can vary considerably. Obviously a dog who is in great demand and siring a number of dogs who are very much to the fore in awards will cost a lot more than a lesser known dog. It must, however, be understood that the owner of the stud dog has the right to refuse to allow his dog to mate your bitch if for any reason he does not consider that she (or even you) are suitable to rear stock sired by his famous stud dog. Alternatively, the dog may have been heavily booked prior to your enquiry being made.

However, assuming that the bitch is accepted and a mating effected, you must then pay the necessary fee.

It is interesting to note that in 1891, Champion Ormskirk Amazement, whose parents had between them been sold for £1,250, was at stud for a fee of five guineas, Ormskirk Chriss at seven guineas, and Ormskirk Curson, only two guineas.

Should the bitch prove not to be in whelp, it is customary for her to be given a free service at her next season. This is purely an agreement between the two parties, however, and is not your right. The dog may for instance, have been sold overseas in the meantime.

WHELPING

You then wait sixty-three days before the puppies are born. It is not unusual, however, for a 'maiden' bitch (a bitch who has not previously had a litter) to have her puppies three or four days before the date on which they are due. It is, therefore, advisable to take precautions and make provisions for this eventuality. During the days prior to the litter being born, take care not to over-exercise the bitch – gentle exercise is good, but long walks are not advisable. In fact, I like my bitches to have a kennel with the door left open so that they can rest or take a walk whenever they feel inclined to.

Extra calcium with Vitamin D should be given at this time and an increase of meat rather than meal will help. In the early stages it is usual for the expectant mother to be extremely hungry; this often lasts until about four weeks before the puppies are due, when there is sometimes a period when one has to tempt her to eat by offering her tasty morsels, (especially during hot weather). If all is well, this does not normally last long, nor does it upset the bitch. You may think that I am very casual about the expectant mother, but I can assure you that I am not. I watch most carefully for any signs which may indicate that something is wrong. One thing I am against is interference with nature, and the longer I live the more I realise what a mistake this can be.

At the first sign that all is not well, I contact my vet immediately. I consider that both at the time of the actual whelping and during the 'waiting' period, a little knowledge can be a dangerous thing and expert advice is a must.

In many cases the actual whelping is straightforward. Most Collie bitches are born with a strong maternal instinct, possibly due to the nature of the work for which they are so well equipped. The first indication of the family is usually that food will be rejected and a 'far away' look will appear in the eye of the expectant mother. She will become restless and will wander around, and if allowed, will make beds in remote places. I consider this to be the time to take and keep her in the whelping kennel. Allow her to move around until the moment she shows signs of the actual labour. This is when I usually invite her to take to her bed.

The whelping box should be already prepared for this moment. An important point to remember is that when scrubbing it out, do not use disinfectant of any form since there is a danger of puppies inhaling the vapour. I recommend ordinary washing soda and boiling water. Allow plenty of time for the box to dry and then cover it with layers of newspapers, which are easy to change and dispose of.

When the bitch is settled in her kennel, wait for the contractions to begin; they may vary, but become gradually stronger and regular. The water is broken during one of these. When this happens there will be a wetness tinged with blood in the whelping box; do not let this disturb or worry you, and do not fuss. 'Mum' will require calmness and reassurance from you at this time. Before very long you should see your first 'home bred' pups.

In the main, Collies do not want you to handle the babies when they are first born. If all goes well and the contractions do not go on for too long before results appear, leave well alone. Make sure that the afterbirths come away. It is a good idea, even if the birth is completely normal, to have your vet check up that everything is clear, otherwise you may have trouble in store.

The puppies should be born head-first, and as the head is larger than the body, once this has appeared and the bitch continues to strain, the entire puppy enclosed in a sac should soon make an appearance. Collies usually release the puppy from the sac at once, but if not, then you must be prepared to do this. A pair of scissors (which must be sterilised) should be used. A quick snip is all that is needed to open the sac. The puppy is attached by the umbilical cord to the afterbirth (or placenta), and it can happen that when the bitch is trying to nibble the cord she may bite too closely to the navel of the puppy. Care must be taken to ensure that this does not happen. If, however, the bitch does not release the puppy from the cord it is up to you to do this yourself. This, again, is done with sterilised scissors. Care must be taken to allow at least 2½ inches from the navel of the puppy. I would like to stress that I prefer to let my bitches follow their normal instincts as much as possible in this respect.

Concerning the afterbirth, some breeders allow the bitch to consume this since they consider it gives strength to the bitch; others try to prevent her doing this as she may be sick. I think that one has to know the individual bitch to decide upon this. Equally important, do not be too anxious to assist the puppies into this world. Often damage is done to both mother and family in this manner, and this is often the cause of an umbilical hernia. It is not uncommon for the bitch to rest and cuddle the first born whilst awaiting the rest of the litter. She may even have a sleep, as the birth can be exhausting. She may require to rest and take a drink, perhaps a little warm milk or egg and milk. On the other hand, I have on one occasion known a litter of five to be born in less than half an hour, but this is unusual.

It is surprising how quickly the puppies will learn how and where to feed. Once out of the sac and washed by mum, they will squirm and wriggle to a teat and continue to feed and thrive from that moment onwards.

As in all things, there is always the unexpected which can and does happen. Sometimes one may get a breech puppy, that is to say, a puppy is born hind-legs-first. The difficulty is when the head becomes lodged. It is not very wise for the inexperienced to attempt to assist, but in the event of the vet not being available, it is necessary for something to be done. The only thing to do is gently to take, in a piece of sterilised lint or similar material, the hind-legs of the puppy and as much of the body as is available and pull *very, very gently* and carefully at the same time as the bitch strains.

One should always have warm towels on hand with which one can rub any puppy who does not appear to respond to his mother's licking; a brisk rub can often work wonders with such a puppy. Another way to aid a puppy which does not seem to be completely alive is to breathe deeply into its lungs.

Many people struggle along with puppies who are not strong and do not seem to grow and thrive. In most cases if one has these poor little mites, in an otherwise healthy litter, it is better to have them put to sleep, since so often they upset the bitch with their endless crying and she does not relax and get on with the business of rearing the rest of the litter. It often happens that such puppies grow up, if indeed they survive, to be unhealthy animals which require a good deal of medical attention. I would like to emphasise that I do not mean a *small* puppy should be put to sleep; this is quite a different thing, since a puppy who is a little smaller than the rest of the litter often catches up and can even be larger than the rest of the litter when fully grown. His size may only be due to worm infestation and after worming he will rapidly grow. It is the 'squeakers' to which I refer; this sound one learns to recognise and it is one to be dreaded. The most beautiful sound to be heard is that of a contented litter all feeding at the 'milk bar' and watching them fall asleep one by one.

I always consider that absolute peace is positively essential for my nursing mothers, and do not allow anyone to see my puppies when they are very young. Another thing which I do not allow is any dogs going near the bitch's kennel. The protective instinct is very strong at this particular time, and in fairness to all, I think only her closest friends should attend her. I find that having many visitors upsets her, and she gets very worried by their presence.

In cold weather the use of an infra-red lamp is of great help to the babies in the early days of their life, but its use should be gradually cut down as they become older. I do not believe in the use of such a lamp to excess, since a Collie is by nature a hardy dog and should be kept that way as much as possible.

If one has the misfortune to have to hand-rear a litter, the use of an infra-red lamp is absolutely essential, and the feeding of the puppies should be done under the supervision of a vet since too much or too little food can be fatal.

If one is faced with this very difficult problem, a very good idea is to obtain the services of a foster mother. By this I mean, of course, a bitch who has happened to have an unwanted litter (not necessarily a Collie). Her owner may be willing to lend the bitch to you, or you may entrust your precious puppies to the owner of the bitch.

Great care has to be taken that the foster mother does not take exception to these puppies when transferring them to her. Assuming that all goes well, however, this is a very much easier method than having to hand-rear, and usually very much more satisfactory.

THE YOUNG PUPPIES

We will now assume that all is well and you have a strong healthy litter and a nursing mother who takes good care of the family, keeping them clean and well fed; it is up to you to see that she is kept the same way, either on clean newspapers or on clean blankets (straw can be dangerous, as the family can get 'lost' in it). Good wholesome food is essential for the first two days after whelping, and the bitch should have light nourishing food such as milk with an egg beaten into it, puppy milk, baby foods and milk puddings. All these foods I prefer to give with the chill taken off and in small quantities at regular intervals; glucose can be added with advantage. Following this period, a high ration of fresh meat should be given and the calcium and vitamins

A proud mother with her nine babies.

should be continued.

If you intend to remove the dew-claws and the dew-claws if any, on the hind-legs, these must be removed between the fourth and the tenth day. I sometimes wonder if this is worth the upset as Collies can become very distressed about this being done even if the bitch has been taken away whilst the task is undertaken. If you have not done this removal before it is as well to seek the advice of an experienced breeder or if this is not possible to have your vet attend to it.

You will have noticed, when grooming prior to whelping, that all the hair from around the bitch's teats has come away. You will now find that slowly the bitch will lose her coat and will eventually look quite naked, hardly having any coat at all. Do not worry about this; it is quite natural and she will grow her new coat again after her maternal duties are accomplished.

Please do see that the puppies' toe nails are kept short so that they do not cause too much discomfort to their mother whilst they are feeding from her. These grow very quickly and are very sharp and can give a very nasty scratch.

Do not be surprised if the bitch refuses to leave the puppies of her own volition during the first few days: she will be very protective towards them and you may have to make her go out to relieve herself and to take a little exercise. She will soon settle down and take things more calmly, and will gradually leave them for longer periods and ask to be allowed out for exercise. This is quite in order as long as the puppies are warm and well fed, and in most instances they will be sleeping. Puppies are so like young babies; they cry when hungry, and after feeding, they sleep. As they grow and their eyes begin to open (usually between ten and fourteen days after birth), to sit and watch them is, to me, sheer joy.

Soon the puppies will be looking for food. My puppies are usually eating very finely minced lean meat by the time they are three weeks old. After this they go on to a variety of things since I feel that, whilst having four or five meals per day, this variety is essential. Many people use dried milk foods, baby foods, baby rusks, and preparations intended specifically for puppies. These are all good and the main thing to remember is to feed at regular times with good wholesome food in clean dishes. Never leave left-over food about or allow food to be available at all times, and do not over-feed or on the other hand, starve your puppies.

You may find that your bitch regurgitates her food for the puppies; this is a way that nature provides pre-digested food, and a good mother will do this for her young. It is then up to you to see that your bitch is given enough food to supply her own needs, keeping her away from the family until her meal has been fully digested.

Allow the puppies to go outside, but when they show signs of having tired of playing, put them back inside to sleep. Do not let them lie on damp or cold ground. In addition, do not allow them to soil their sleeping quarters, and you will be surprised how soon they will become house-trained.

Most puppies are infested with round worms, and they will require worming. There are several good preparations on the market for this purpose, some of which, if found to be necessary, can be given to the puppy as early as three or four weeks old. I do not as a rule worm my puppies until they are about six weeks old, and then I repeat the treatment after another ten days. After this the puppies, who should be by now completely self supporting, will soon be ready to go to their new homes; I suggest that eight weeks is a suitable age for them to leave.

Please consider having the puppies inoculated when they are old enough. I am well aware of the questions which have arisen lately regarding this, but I am still in favour, having seen too much distress and loss of puppies in the days before inoculation came into being.

CHOICE OF PUPPIES TO RETAIN

I can never see the purpose of breeding a litter unless it is desired to retain something for oneself, so we are now back with the problem of choice. I usually make my own choice whilst the puppies are still wet from being born, if you are able to recognise their shape at this time. They will finish, as grown dogs, as the quality they are when first born, but will alter many times in between. Naturally, colour of eyes and dentition cannot be assessed at this time, but I seldom have second thoughts about choice. Consider keeping two puppies, if possible, as two are much easier to rear, and certainly much more fun to watch.

DIET

Common sense is all that is now required, and a sensible diet containing plenty of protein. My youngsters have four meals a day, basically two milk and two meat at this age, with of course calcium and cod-liver oil or some similar source of vitamins. These days, many people rely on processed and tinned meals and the prepared foods. I am afraid that I am still old-fashioned enough to prefer to use fresh butcher's meat wherever possible, and only in emergencies do I use the other varieties. I am still lucky enough to be able to buy fresh eggs from hens who range free. When I was young and we had our own hens, the eggs for the dogs were taken out of the day's collection before any went to the house, and three cows provided the milk for us and this was allocated in the same manner as the eggs (much to the annoyance of my mother, who was not dog-minded). In later years, five goats were kept to provide the milk for the dogs.

Here is a typical puppy's diet, as a guide to feeding.

6–12 weeks
Breakfast: Cereal and milk with egg.
Lunch: Meat, either raw or cooked, with either brown bread or small puppy meal.
Tea: Milk pudding.
Dinner: Same as lunch, alternating variety of bread and puppy meal and variety of meat.
Supper: Drink of milk with glucose added.

3–6 months
Breakfast: Cereal with milk or egg and milk.
Lunch: Meat either cooked or raw.
Dinner: Meat with brown bread or puppy meal.

At this age I introduce a few hard biscuits to assist teething and give large marrow bones which cannot splinter. These bones must *never* be left out in runs at night since they will encourage vermin.

6–12 months
Breakfast: Cereal and milk or egg and milk.
Lunch: Meat in some form either raw or cooked or any of the specially prepared meats.
Dinner: Meal soaked in gravy of cooked meat and of course, the cooked meat.

Adult Dogs
As the 6–12-month diet, except without the lunch. In all cases I give marrow bones and hard biscuits, as I do not believe in dogs being fed soft foods only – I like them to have to use their teeth.

From these diets it will be seen that no mention is made of white bread. This should never be used in the feeding of dogs. It is generally believed that the mineral parts of the wheat, mainly phosphate, are removed with the bran during the milling process. These are absolutely essential for bone, formation of teeth, and brain development. Many years ago tests were carried out; part of a litter was fed on white bread and the other half on brown bread. At the end of the experiment, the puppies fed on white bread were very much smaller than those which had been fed on brown bread, and they showed a definite tendency towards rickets. For this reason alone, it is advisable to purchase meal

Puppies a few weeks old.

which has been made with brown flour and not white, even though this meal may prove to be slightly more expensive than the others.

CONCLUDING POINTS
This covers most aspects of the rearing of the puppies; some points to remember are as follows.

Do not over-exercise your puppies. This can be as harmful as lack of exercise.

Never put any Collie young or old to bed if he is wet; dry him down first.

I am not, in general, in favour of puppies being dragged around on leads too early, as shoulders can be spoilt by this. However, do not wait until he or she is entered for his first show before taking him out into traffic and crowds, or you will have a very frightened and upset Collie. At a show quite recently, I saw a young girl with a dog who would not even walk on a lead. It escaped and was caught by spectators just as it was dashing out of the show in terror. Please do not allow this kind of thing to happen.

8 General Care

The general care of the Collie is really no more difficult than that of any other domestic animal. An adult dog requires a fair amount of exercise to keep him fit and healthy – I don't mean just a short walk round the block; a Collie loves to gallop, and this is a thing which gives enormous pleasure to the dog and is good to watch by his owner. I consider all Collies should be given the opportunity to stretch their limbs in this way; road walking on a lead helps too, and at the same time gets the dog used to traffic and people.

The Collie loves to be well kept; my own dogs queue up to be groomed and will, if allowed, push one another aside in order that they may be attended to first. There is a wide choice of grooming tools. Some people use a nylon brush, but my own choice, however, is a wire or whalebone brush, (the latter not very easily purchased in these modern times). The coat should be vigorously brushed, if possible every day, taking the hair against the natural trend of growth and then brushing it back again. The use of a comb is not very necessary, other than to clean the brush and, of course, for feathering etc. A healthy coat is the result of regular grooming, and will have that 'extra sparkle' about it.

Washing should not be undertaken too often, as it tends to destroy the natural harshness. A soft fluffy coat will be the result of too much bathing. It is, however, a good idea to bath your Collie when he starts to cast his coat. It will bring the already-loose coat out much more speedily, remove the dirt at the same time, and will give a clean skin, which must surely help to grow a clean healthy new coat. When you decide to do this, choose a warm sunny day with, if possible, a slight breeze.

Wet the dog very thoroughly – you may find this difficult, as a weather-resisting coat such as that of the Collie tends to repel the water, but one must persevere. Apply one of the many well-known shampoos, taking care to avoid this or water getting into the dog's ears and eyes. Rub well into the coat until a rich lather ensues, then rinse. If the dog is very dirty, repeat the process. Finally, rinse well, making sure that all traces of shampoo have been removed completely. Please do not put your dog into very hot water; a simple way to test the temperature is to put your elbow into the water. If it is too hot for your elbow, don't put the dog in until the water has been cooled down. It is a good idea to have someone to help you with this operation, since a shake from a well-sodden Collie at the wrong time results in you being soaked too! When you have removed the dog from the water (and are not in your own bathroom!) allow him to shake himself. A great deal of water will be dispersed in this way, and a good rub with clean dry towels should follow. If you do not happen to have a hand drier, allow him to run about outside for a short time, then take a brush and comb and literally brush him dry. Whilst you are brushing, the sun and the wind will soon do their work; dead hair will come out as you do this, and you must comb as well as brush to remove the old coat.

We are very fortunate in this country in that we are not plagued with ticks and fleas, as are many other countries. I do not think we realise that in quite a number of countries, ticks are a serious menace, and it can be quite impossible at certain times of the year to allow dogs to walk on any grass. It is not uncommon for dogs and cats to wear collars which are specially treated to guard against this pest. At the same time, some people consider that these collars can be a health risk to the animals who wear them.

Nails should be kept short. If sufficient exercise is given on hard surfaces, this will be taken care of. If not, there is an excellent type of clipper which does this trimming quickly and without pain or discomfort to the dog. The one I use is made in the United States of America and is illustrated.

Do take extreme care not to cut beyond the quick which can easily be felt when clipping. Keep the hair between the pads short, since long hair will retain moisture in wet weather and can cause sore feet.

Getting the correct ear carriage seems to cause a great deal of

FIGURE 10: Nail Clippers.

trouble. I can never understand why this is so. If a Collie puppy shows a tendency towards prick ears (erect ears) a light grease should be applied at once. Vaseline, glycerine, olive oil, or any light grease of this nature, may be used. This grease should be applied to the top of the ear on the inside only as soon as any sign of prick ears is observed. If this is done immediately and the ear is gently rolled so that the grease will be absorbed, then after a few days the ear should fall into a natural fold. If however, these prick ears are not dealt with and stand erect for some length of time you will have difficulty and may not succeed in correcting this fault. Do not forget that when the dog goes to a show, all signs of any grease must be removed, and of course, weights, if these have been used.

It is surprising what methods are used to try to get ears down: many people use things like kaolin or wool fat and (to my horror) dip the ears in sand or some gritty substance which adheres to the grease and makes the ear heavier and so fall in the correct manner. This is all very well, but I think the danger of grit getting into the eyes of the dog from this method is far too great. Further, when removing the substance, it is likely that you will remove some of the hair as well and so make the ear lighter than before. Another method to correct faulty ears is this: apply sticking plaster into which a small lead weight has been fastened; this will certainly bring the ears down, but a short time after its removal the ear may become erect again. Chewing gum can also be seen attached to the ears of many Collies, usually with the same result as the lead weight and sticking plaster.

In spite of all this, I still consider that prick ears are easier to get down than low ears are to get up to the correct position. These low ears are usually on the large side and not really very well placed; the only suggestions I can make for these cases are to trim off as much hair as possible and then try to keep the dog somewhere where he has to look up to see what is going on around him. In either situation, prick or low ears, attention should be given as soon as it is perceived that all is not as it should be – don't wait until tomorrow! We all know and accept that ears will do the most fantastic things whilst the dog is teething. This is the time when they go up and they should be dealt with immediately.

Do not under any circumstances allow any of these corrective medicaments to enter the ear itself or you will be laying on trouble for the dog and, of course, yourself.

It is as well to treat your dog for worms occasionally; about once a year is good practice. It is a wise precaution, as dogs can suffer from these pests without showing any obvious signs of infestation. There are many types of worms, the most common being round worms, which are found in puppies and young dogs, and tape worms, usually found in older dogs. It is as well to consult your vet who will tell you what and how much to give of the prescribed vermifuge. Never exceed the amount stated by your vet; overdoses can prove extremely dangerous.

Any dog can pick up fleas whilst out for his daily walk, so always be on the lookout for the odd 'visitor'; he too can be the host for worms. If your dog is as he should be, habitually clean, you will soon know if fleas are present, since he will scratch or bite himself continually until he is free of them. Dusting your dog with one of the appropriate powders, or even bathing, using a specially prepared medicated shampoo, will soon eradicate fleas or lice. Remember to treat bedding and kennels as well as your dog, or re-infestation will occur.

Teeth will be kept clean and gums healthy if a large marrow bone is given once in a while. This *must* be given *raw*. Once cooked, bones are likely to splinter. *Never* allow your Collie to have chicken or chop bones, or any bones of that category; they are all likely to splinter, and can cause untold damage which could even prove to be fatal.

TRAINING

I have not mentioned training at length, as I do not think that Collies require a great deal. In my experience they soon learn what is required of them and do their best to please. I never consciously teach my dogs to do anything other than the ringcraft. They seem to anticipate my thoughts. To quote one small example of this, they never jump on to the seat of a car, bus or train until I have placed a sheet or blanket down for them to lie on.

We all know that the Collie has a natural ability to work, and there are several show dogs whom I know, who regularly work both sheep and cattle on the farms where they live. Unfortunately, not many Collies have the chance to show their ability in this direction. I always feel that the Collie likes to use his brains in the work he does, rather than be made to do things. We have had at least one Rough Collie who was a bench champion and distinguished herself in Obedience – Mr Frank Mitchell's Rifflesee Reward of Glenmist.

I have never been very keen on Obedience work, however, as I feel that a great deal of monotony in training is not suited to the temperament of the Collie. Having seen in America a top handler dealing with a dog (not a Collie) who would not walk on a certain flooring, I became more convinced than ever that Obedience work was not for me or my Collies.

In all fairness though, I should state that at this same 'passing-out' evening (where the dogs have reached a certain grade of their initial training), the highest number of marks for novice handlers and their dogs went to the nine-year-old daughter of Marian Durholz, with a Rough Collie puppy bitch; Marian herself came out with the overall highest mark of the evening, with a young Smooth dog puppy. Both of these, being well-known winners on the bench, seemed to enjoy themselves thoroughly.

My own idea of training is to have a complete understanding with my dogs. I think they know and understand me better than anyone else and if I am not well or upset it is surprising how they seem to understand; a cold wet nose will be thrust into my hand or a paw will gently arrive in my lap. Never scold and at the same time laugh – if you have to admonish, let the dog see that you mean it. In the same way, do not hesitate to praise if praise is due. In that way, you will soon earn the respect of your Collie.

9 Showing

I am describing in this chapter the types of shows which are held, the qualifications needed to make your dog a Champion, and also various aspects of judging in this country and on the continent. Following this, I have then tried to explain the procedure for showing your dog, right up to the moment he is in the show ring being judged.

Apart from the preparation of the Rough Collie, upon which I must dwell, the remarks and all things relative to showing are basically the same for all dogs.

The Kennel Club is the governing body in all matters relating to dog shows in the United Kingdom, and no show can be held without the permission of the Kennel Club. A licence to hold a show has to be obtained by the show promoters from the Kennel Club and this has to be held under the rules of the Kennel Club applicable to the type of show.

The Championship Show is a show which is open to all exhibitors, where Challenge Certificates can be awarded and Champions can be exhibited.

An Open Show is also open to all exhibitors, but there are no Challenge Certificates on offer.

A Limited or Sanction Show is limited to members of the Club or Society promoting the show.

The Kennel Club will be pleased to supply Regulations concerning these shows, on request to the Secretary of the Kennel Club, 1 Clarges Street, London W1Y 8AB.

It is a good idea to make oneself familiar with the Rules and Regulations of the Kennel Club in all matters applying to dog shows.

A Challenge Certificate is awarded to the best of each sex in each breed where Challenge Certificates are on offer for that breed. A Challenge Certificate is an award which counts towards the making of a Champion. To become a Champion, a dog must win three Kennel Club Challenge Certificates under three different judges at three different Championship Shows. However, at least one Challenge Certificate must be won after the dog has reached the age of one year.

Matches may be held in this country by permission of the Kennel Club only; these may be inter-club, or held in conjunction with another club; they are usually of a very friendly nature, and no prize money is given. In the main, these are a social gathering, and are generally held to help stimulate interest in the clubs.

Schedules of the various shows can be obtained free of charge from the secretary whose name and address can be found in the advertisement columns of the canine magazines *Our Dogs* and *Dog World* (available on subscription) or from the *Kennel Gazette*, which is purchased direct from the Kennel Club.

Definitions of classes are printed at the beginning of every schedule, and you should read these very carefully before completing your entry form.

If the show is confined to members only of a society, please do not forget to add your subscription to the entrance fee.

If you decide to join any of the breed clubs, you will be entitled to take part in all the club's activities, i.e. social evenings, club meetings, etc., as well as competing for trophies or special prizes which may be confined to that club or society.

You can also discuss any problems you have with other members of the club; most of the senior members will be willing to give you the benefit of their experience.

When showing and judging dogs, one meets people from all walks of life. It is amazing how easily this common interest brings together people of varying trades and professions.

One of the most colourful characters I remember was Albert Payson Terhune, whose many books about dogs, particularly Collies, have been world-famous; whilst in America I learnt that a Memorial Fund has been raised to perpetuate the memory of this great man and his Collies, many of whom were Champions and bore the prefix 'Sunnybank'. One of my most treasured possessions is a photograph of Champion Sunnybank Sigurd and his master, given to my father when Mr Terhune visited the Laund Kennel at Rawtenstall.

Another name which comes to mind when thinking of people in the public eye associated with Collies is Professor Duncan, with his performing Collies. Whilst I have always had doubts about performing animals, having met Professor Duncan and being taken back-stage to see the dogs, I am sure that these are exceptions to what one hears of animals being cruelly treated; Professor Duncan's Collies were a very happy bunch and obviously devoted to their trainer.

It was after this visit that my father was persuaded to sell one of our sable-and-white dogs to become the clown of the act. This dog threw himself wholeheartedly into his new way of life, learning new tricks and becoming the star turn of the act, with his obvious enjoyment and changes of expression causing great amusement. This, incidentally, surely disproves the theory that the exhibition Collie lacks brains. I would like to deny the common misconception that because the Collie has a refined head he cannot have much room for brains. Given the opportunity to show his skill and ability, the modern exhibition Collie will hold his own with any breed of dog, and is of outstanding intelligence. At the same time I would also like to deny the theory that Collies can be sly and treacherous. Having been brought up surrounded by a Kennel containing some fifty Collies, I was always given free run of the Kennels. I have never been bitten by a Collie. One sometimes hears stories of someone being bitten by a Collie, but when the truth is eventually revealed, invariably the dog in question has not been a pure-bred Collie, but a Collie 'type' on some remote farm. In any case, the dog is really protecting his property and doing the job for which he is intended.

JUDGING

A certain amount of experience has to be gained before any thoughts of judging should be considered. Most judges start by judging at the smaller shows where invaluable experience can be gained, later graduating to Open Shows. It is after the experience gained at these shows, according to the ability shown, that a judge may be chosen for inclusion in the Breed Club's list of judges.

Championship Show Judges must be approved by the Kennel Club after recommendations have been received from the Breed Society and the Breed Council. A unified judges list is compiled by the Breed Council from the recommendations supplied by the Breed Clubs. A great deal of care goes into the selection of Championship Show Judges, as they will carry a great deal of responsibility in furthering the advancement of the breed. A questionnaire is received by all judges who have been invited to judge the breed at a Championship Show for the first time. The questions cover: experience, knowledge of the breed, number of dogs owned or bred, previous judging experience, etc. According to the answers received, judges are selected or declined by the Kennel Club.

If at some time you should aspire to judging, be certain that you have the knowledge and experience as well as a natural eye for a good dog. This latter is absolutely essential. If one does not possess an eye for a dog, all the learning and tuition will have been wasted.

From the ring-side it is so easy to criticise. Standing in the ring to judge dogs for the first time can be a terrifying experience. One is quite alone, with no one to discuss the relative merits and failings of the dogs, so you must decide upon a plan of campaign.

When I was confronted with this situation at the age of nineteen, I was seized by terror. I suddenly hit upon the plan of moving the dogs round the ring two or three times and I soon became so engrossed that

I forgot my fright and got on with the job in hand, which eventually I enjoyed to the full. Once having overcome the shock of your first show, you will find judging an enjoyable task, so long as you forget the faces owned by the exhibitors and concentrate on the dogs. Remember that your decision is final. Whatever anyone else may think, it is *you* who has been asked to judge the dogs and it is *your* opinion that is being sought, not that of someone who might be sitting at the ring-side! After you have completed judging the classes, you may perhaps be confronted by an exhibitor who did not agree with your placings; do not lose your temper, but try to remain completely calm and confidently give your reasons for the order of the winners.

You may, after having gained experience at the smaller shows, be invited to judge your first Championship Show. You will by this time have a great deal more confidence than you had at the outset. Remember always that if you do not consider that any dog is worthy of the title 'Champion', you are at liberty to withhold the Challenge Certificate. In practice this does not happen very often in this breed, owing to the high standard of the exhibits which are now presented, but it is something which should always be borne in mind.

Judging overseas
You may even at some later date be invited to judge overseas; this is a wonderful opportunity which should if at all possible be accepted. My first invitation to judge overseas was a very exciting experience, but one which I undertook with some trepidation, as I was going to a country which I had not had occasion to visit before and whose language was completely unknown to me. I need not have worried, however, since I was met at the airport by two of the most charming people, and the lady who acted as my interpreter throughout my visit was kindness itself – even going to the trouble of selecting a meal from the menu put before me, of which I could not understand a word! All my reports on the show were written out by this lady and translated for the recipients.

The judging of the dogs was again a new experience, as the method used was somewhat different to the one to which I was accustomed. However, I managed to take this in my stride and enjoyed the opportunity of seeing what Collies looked like in another part of the world. I must admit that some of them surprised me. I did, however, find several which pleased me, and soon discovered that when talking about Collies, language difficulties did not really exist. After the show I was invited to celebrate with the winners and losers, and, again through my interpreter, gave the reasons for placing the dogs in what I considered was the order of merit. This was an extremely nice conclusion to the day and further enhanced my impression of the hospitality I received on this my first engagement overseas.

A fortnight later, I again left home to undertake my second overseas appointment, in another country. Having already experienced such wonderful hospitality, I was not surprised to receive the same wonderful kindness and consideration for my comfort and well-being. I was, however, somewhat dismayed when making my final placings at the show, to find the ring almost as full of spectators, trying to attract the attention of the would-be winners, as of competitors! Not surprisingly, I stopped judging and asked my stewards to remove all those 'noise makers' and we finished the judging in silence!

Most countries have their own methods of judging and grading the dogs but usually it works out that one has a best dog and best bitch. It is really only the method by which one achieves this end that is somewhat different. To those of you who may be considering, at this moment, whether or not to accept an overseas engagement, I would say, by all means do – you will undoubtedly enjoy every moment.

Having judged in many countries, I am convinced that Collie people, wherever they happen to live and whether their dogs reach the high standard one would like or not, are a most kind and hospitable 'breed' of their own. Perhaps they take on the nature of the Collie.

The following quotation might have been written with the dog fraternity in mind. It could apply to both judges and exhibitors:

> 'There's so much good in the worst of us
> And so much bad in the best of us
> That it doesn't behove any of us
> To speak ill of the rest of us.'

Judge selection

Various countries, as I have mentioned, have various methods of selecting their judges. For instance, in Scandinavia the method is quite different to that used in the United Kingdom and one must have a knowledge of anatomy, genetics and typology. (I thank Mr Harald Ulltveit-Moe for the information on judging in Scandinavia.)

One is only allowed to judge in Scandinavia after receiving the permission of the Kennel Club of the country concerned, or a specialist club for any breed. After this, being conversant with the rules of the Kennel Club, one has to act as a steward. After you have been a steward on two occasions, the Kennel Club will consider you once again, and you may then be allowed to proceed on to a Judging Panel. Prior to this, however, rigorous practical judging examinations have to be taken. When these first examinations have been completed, you begin your course as part of the Judging Panel, and study genetics and anatomy for six months. After completing these studies, examinations have to be taken in genetics, typology, anatomy and practical judging. After the course on the Judging Panel, you have to be present in the show ring with a judge who is qualified and experienced in the breed you intend judging. You are at liberty to ask questions as to the reasons why the dogs have been placed in any particular order and the judge must give his reasons.

When you have followed the judge for several shows, and if you feel you are competent to begin judging yourself, you then begin to write your own criticism of the dogs; but you are not allowed to talk to the judge whilst doing this particular exercise. The criticism you write has then to be presented to the Kennel Club and the Kennel Club send copies of this to the specialist club and to the person judging at that particular show. Your ability is then assessed from these critiques, and you are told whether you are worthy to judge. After the practical judging, an oral examination has to be taken, conducted by representatives from the specialist club and Kennel Club and also Doctors from the veterinary high schools. When the Kennel Club Education Committee have studied your answers and found that they are correct, you will be granted a certificate which then allows you to judge a particular breed. If the Kennel Club think you may be capable of judging other breeds, you have to follow the judge in the ring as before, but it is not necessary to take the examinations again in anatomy and genetics. Here again, you must obtain the permission from the specialist clubs and Kennel Club before being able to continue in this field.

System of showing dogs in Scandinavia

When you start showing dogs in Norway, it is general to begin with the puppy shows of specialist clubs. These shows are for puppies under fifteen months, and each dog in the show will be given written criticism signed by the judge. The puppies can be shown in puppy classes and the judge can give as many first, second and third prizes as appropriate. A very lovely puppy wins a first prize, and a poorer one, a third.

The dogs who have first prizes then compete in a Winner's Class and are placed first, second, third and fourth. The winner of this competition for the dogs meets the winner of the bitch class, and they then compete for Best of Breed. It is not usual to have money prizes, but most of the clubs award trophies.

When the dog is eight months old you can start to show him at Championship Shows in a Youth Class. In these classes the judge again writes a criticism for each dog and places them. This class is only a quality class, and they can obtain first, second or third prizes. The first-prize winners go on further to a Youth Winner Class, where they are placed first, second, third, fourth and reserve. A judge may think that some of the young dogs are worth a Prize of Honour for very outstanding quality; these dogs go forward to compete against adult dogs for C.C. later in the same show.

In the Open Classes, the dogs must be at least fifteen months. The judging takes place as in the Youth Class; the Open Class is only a quality class, and the dogs are placed first, second or third class categories. The first-prize winners and Youth Dogs who won Prizes of Honour go together to a Winner's Class, competing for the C.C. for each sex. The dogs and bitches compete separately, as in this country. Both C.C.-winning dogs and dogs with Prizes of Honour in the other classes compete in a class known as Best of Breed Class, where the judge chooses his Best of Breed, and second, third and fourth Best of Breed, irrespective of sex. A Prize of Honour indicates that the dog in the judge's opinion is worth a C.C., but only one C.C. is awarded to each sex.

International classes

C.A.C.I.B.s are certificates which are presented only at International Championship Shows. One is awarded for each sex, but these may be withheld if the judge does not consider the exhibits to be of sufficiently outstanding merit. These International Championship Shows are arranged by the Kennel Clubs. For a Collie to become an International Champion, he has to have four C.A.C.I.B.s in three different countries, granted by three different judges. There must be a period of one year between the first and the last C.A.C.I.B., the idea being that the dog must maintain the outstanding quality during the full twelve months.

Another class permitted is the Veteran Class, which is judged in the same way as other classes but with the restriction that dogs are over seven years of age.

A further class to note with interest is the Progeny Class; stud dogs enter with at least five of their progeny, not necessarily from the same litter, but which have won three first prizes in Quality Classes, and two second prizes. They are allowed to compete for a Prize of Honour but the judge is allowed to withhold this.

SHOWING YOUR DOG IN BRITAIN

You cannot show any dog under six months of age, nor can you enter for a show any dog who is not registered at the Kennel Club. If you have purchased your Collie from a breeder who has not registered him, please make sure that at the time of purchase you receive a registration form duly completed and signed by the breeder. You will then fill in your choice of names, your own name and address, and send the fully completed form to the Kennel Club with the appropriate fee.

If you have not received the registration card from the Kennel Club before the entries close for the show you wish to enter, you may still enter, but you must put N.A.F. (name applied for) after the name you have chosen for your dog.

If the dog has already been registered by the breeder, you must then ask him or her to sign a transfer form which must be completed and returned to the Kennel Club with the appropriate fee. If by any chance neither the breeder nor you have any of the relevant forms these may be obtained free of charge from the Kennel Club.

The name of the dog, once registered at the Kennel Club, may not be changed; the only change permitted is the addition of an affix. Most breeders who have their own affix wish to add this to the name of any dogs they may purchase from another breeder. You may, if you desire, apply for an affix which will be used by you only and no other breeder may use this once the fee has been paid and the Kennel Club has granted this right to you.

The sensible thing to do before you start to follow the Championship Shows is to enter your dog for one of the smaller shows. There are many small shows held by the various breed clubs throughout the country. There is a list, with the names and addresses of the Hon. Secretaries, in Appendix 1, page 118.

When filling in the entry form for a show, give the particulars of your dog as shown on the Registration Card, and enter in the classes best suited to your dog. For example, if a Puppy Class is provided and your dog is still a puppy, that is a good choice.

Read the class definitions carefully and enter accordingly. Do send the money with your entries, otherwise they may be returned to you. Remember that the time stated for the closing of entries means just what it says; do not expect the secretary to accept entries sent after that time.

A visit to a show as a spectator often pays dividends; you will then be able to watch how other people handle their dogs, how the judges handle them, and what, in general, is expected of you and your dog.

Most Collies adapt themselves very readily to showing; this is a good thing, as many people only decide to show at the last minute, so that training is limited. My own dogs are trained with showing in mind: from the moment they wear a collar and lead, they always walk on my left side, no matter how many dogs I have with me. (This also has the advantage that it leaves your right hand free.)

The dog should be taught to walk at whatever pace you, his handler, may choose; he should never strain on the lead or hang back. He should stop when you do – and by this I do not mean sit. He will then easily turn to whichever position you wish him to show. It is also an advantage to train your dog to stand quite still when he is being examined by the judge. This is not difficult if you have control over your dog and if you intend to show him, he *should* be under perfect control. There is nothing more trying for a judge than attempting to go over a 'bucking bronco', or even a nervous dog who is reluctant to be handled. In either case it is difficult for the judge to assess the dog.

In the same way, when asked to 'move' your dog, you are to walk him up and down the ring for his movement to be assessed. He must walk briskly to and from the judge in a straight line on a loose lead. In the case of the Rough and Smooth Collie, you must teach your exhibit to stand and show his ears. A good way to teach this is to carry some tit-bit in your pocket and from time to time feed him with a tasty morsel, so that when the judge is looking at him, your dog will stand to attention with his ears in the correct position. Above all, make sure that he will pay attention to you and not be growling or snarling at the dog standing next to him.

Keep one eye on the judge and one on your dog. If there is a large number of dogs in the ring, both you and your dog can relax after being examined by the judge, but when all the other dogs have been shown, you must keep your dog on show to the best advantage until the final awards have been made.

The Collie Club Challenge Trophy

For best in all classes (Rough or Smooth).
Open to all. Not to be won outright.

When first presented, the Collie Club Challenge Trophy was valued at 60 guineas; its present-day value is around £1,000. It was awarded for the Best in all Classes, and if won by a non-member of the Collie Club, security had to be given. With this trophy a Collie Club Silver Medal (valued at £1 11s 6d) was presented. A Collie Club Bronze Medal (valued at 10s 6d) was also presented to the breeder (if known) of the dog or bitch winning the trophy, except in the case when such a breeder had already received a Club Medal as Exhibitor or Breeder of such a dog or bitch.

This trophy was originally the property of the Collie Club, but when the Collie Club, Northern Collie Club, the Rough Blue Merle Club and the Smooth Collie Club were incorporated, the name given was the British Collie Club and this is one of the oldest breed clubs. Today the trophy is awarded to the Best in Show at the annual Championship Show of the British Collie Club and the medals are no longer given.

I have often noticed that many people attending the annual Championship Show are interested in looking at the beautiful trophy in order to see just who it has been awarded to. For this purpose I am setting out in Appendix 3, page 122, the names of the winners from the commencement in 1886 up to World War I. (To list the winners onwards from this date would be rather a lengthy business.)

The British Collie Club Challenge Trophy.

10 Basic Preparation

There is, for me, a great deal of pleasure in preparing a Collie for the show ring. It is no use being in a hurry if you are going to do the job properly. If your dog has got very dirty you may have to wash his mane and frill, and legs and feet. If this is the case, it should be done a day or two prior to the show so that there will not be the softness of coat which usually follows washing.

I usually start with the legs and feet; if any toe nails have grown so that they spoil the appearance of the feet, they should be clipped as described earlier. The hair between the pads should be taken out with a sharp pair of blunt-ended scissors. (Never use pointed ends because if the dog should move, the ends could run into his foot.) Next trim the hair from between the toes with a trimming knife – not scissors, as they would leave the foot looking shorn. The feet should now look neat and tidy and of good shape.

The hocks are the next consideration; below these, most Collies grow a little soft fluffy hair. Take the hind leg in your left hand and comb this hair up. Next take a pair of scissors with long blades and with one even cut, remove the surplus hair. Finish off with a trimming knife. Please do not remove all the hair, as this can give a bad impression, just as much as does clipping with clippers or cutting with a small pair of scissors – a smooth finish is required to give the 'untouched' look. I have always been taught that the art of trimming a Collie is to make it look as though it has not been trimmed.

The teeth should be cleaned if necessary, and any tartar removed. If the dog has been given hard biscuits or large bones, the teeth should be healthy and not require cleaning. If this is not the case and the teeth have become badly scaled, it may be necessary for you to have them dealt with professionally, since unless one is used to doing this, considerable discomfort can be caused to the dog. It is a good idea to clean the teeth once in a while in any case, as one would clean one's own teeth.

The head and ears now require attention. All grease or weights must be removed from the ears before entering the ring or you may be disqualified or fined. If you have noticed that some soft fluffy hair has grown at the base of the ears, you may gently remove this by finger and thumb or by the careful use of your fine trimming knife. Do not take hair from the tips of the ears as you may find that the ears will go up;

only the long untidy hairs should be removed. Never use clippers or take too much hair from behind the ears, as this will give the appearance of horns instead of ears and a hard expression and outlook will result.

To give advice on the trimming of the head is not easy as, like human beings, no two dogs are alike. Each requires different treatment. You can, with a very fine comb, remove any surplus hair from the sides of the cheeks. You may also remove surplus hair from around the throat in the same way. If, however, your exhibit's head happens to be on the 'fine' side, this feature would be accentuated by the trimming and would not be a good idea. On the other hand, a coarse-headed dog would be improved.

The coat is the next detail to receive attention. Pour about an eggcupful of methylated or surgical spirit into a bucketful of warm water, then immerse a large sponge in this solution. Wring it out, and sponge the coat all over, until the coat is fairly damp. You must now have two clean towels ready. With the first one rub the dog vigorously. This will remove most of the moisture; the second towel will dry the coat. Your dog will now look much cleaner.

Next, take the brush, and from the hind-quarters brush the coat in the opposite way to growth and then back again. Work over the entire coat in this manner; do not at this stage worry about the lay of the coat. When the frill and other white areas are what I call 'damp dry', dust on your whitening powder. This may be starch, talcum powder, french chalk, chalk block, or any of the specially prepared powders for this purpose. Take care not to allow any of this to blow into the dog's eyes and ears.

Go all over the dog's coat with your brush; for the breechings, tail and feathering, use your comb as well. Pay particular attention to the area behind the ears. Now brush out the surplus powder; if your dog is tri-colour, make sure that you have not allowed any of the powder to get into the black, as that will spoil the effect of the colouring. Finally, give a quick polish of the head to remove any traces of white (especially if your dog has a white blaze which you have whitened).

All this should be done before you get to the show so that upon arrival your Collie should only require 'touching up'. Any white feet which have become soiled during the journey can be quickly cleaned, and a quick freshen-up should be all that is required when actually at the show. It is not advisable on any account to leave trimming, in any shape or form, to be done at the show. Do not use any kind of lacquer on the coat of your Collie. This is not only against Kennel Club regulations, but it does absolutely nothing for the coat.

11 Show Day

Leave yourself ample time to complete the journey from home to the show venue. Remember to leave an extra half an hour or so for the long queue you may encounter as you approach the show, if the event is one of the large championship shows. This even applies for a small show, if it takes place in a busy town. If you arrive at the show all flustered, you will only transmit your anxiety to your dog, who will not give of his best when you have to rush into the ring.

Remember to take a bowl so that you can supply him with a drink of water on arrival. It is a good idea to have a bottle of water with you, as this will save you having to fetch water from an always-distant source.

Let us assume that it is a benched show, and that you have a few minutes in hand. Put your Collie on his bench and fasten him securely with a bench chain, obtained for this purpose from any pet shop. (If you do not happen to have a chain with you, these can usually be purchased from a stand at the show.) It is not uncommon for some Collies to have a habit of biting through their leads in their desire to follow their owners, so this is a safeguard. Do not, however, present your Collie wearing a thick or unsightly collar and lead when you take him into the ring. A fine lead which will not spoil the dog's 'collar' or detract from the picture is advisable. After fastening your Collie, stay with him for a while, so that he is accustomed to the bench where he must spend the whole day except for the time you require to prepare him and being judged. He should not be absent from his bench for more than fifteen minutes at any other time during the day.

Find out which is the Collie ring; watch and listen for an announcement about the commencement of judging. When advised, proceed to the ring to await your classes; keep your dog close to you and do not let him interfere with any other dogs. The Ring Steward will give you your Ring Number, and will tell you where you should stand when first you enter the ring. Whilst in the ring, you must obey without question any instructions given by the Judge or Ring Stewards.

Showing dogs is great fun; it is also heart-breaking and expensive, but if you have a really good dog who is 'top-dog material', and you present and handle him really well, you *will* eventually get him to the top if you persevere. It is a waste of time and money to try to do this with an inferior Collie, since there are too many really high-class exhibits on the benches today; competition is far too keen to allow anyone to win with a second-rate animal. This is a breed where absolute novices can and do win top honours, but try always to be a good loser, and above all do not take out your bad temper on your Collie! (Yes, this does happen.) On the whole the shows are firstly for the exhibition of the dogs, and secondly, social gatherings where one meets and chats with one's fellow exhibitors and friends.

Not too long ago, I was one of a party of five who made a four-hundred-mile round trip to a certain show. We were an optimistic crowd and had with us a bottle of champagne for our celebration. The dogs did not win, but we opened the bottle all the same in the bedroom of the hotel. Enlivened by its journey, the cork hit the ceiling. You can guess the rest, but we did manage a sip each!

There is nothing quite so thrilling as winning your first Challenge Certificate. No matter how many you eventually win, that magic is never lost.

12 The Smooth Collie

I cannot write a chapter on Smooth Collies without expressing my delight at the number of really beautiful Smooth Collies presented to me when I was honoured to judge this breed at the Maryland Kennel Club Show in November 1969. Most of these Collies possessed such beautiful bone, legs and feet and that lovely body so essential to a Smooth Collie. It was indeed my pleasure and privilege to see these beautiful dogs, and it was nice to see such delightful specimens in a country other than their homeland.

The Smooth Collie is, in my opinion, one of the most beautiful of the smooth-coated breeds. As a companion they have all the attributes of the Rough Collie, and yet not the heavy coat; this surely is an advantage in the wet weather which we experience so much in this country, and this perhaps makes them more acceptable as a house dog. Youngsters are easy to rear and easy to train; they are affectionate and yet very good guards. (The fact that they are so keen-eared makes them unbeatable in this respect.) Despite the above factors, most people seem to prefer the glamour of the Rough, and so the Smooth does not gain the popularity he so richly deserves. In consequence not as many shows cater for the Smooths, and sometimes the quality of the breed suffers as a result.

One wonders if, had Queen Victoria taken an interest in the Smooth instead of the Rough Collie, their popularity might have been increased so that they might in fact have held the place the Roughs occupy today.

THE EARLY HISTORY

The Smooth Collie owes a great deal to Mr T. B. Swinburne, one of the earliest supporters. His Tri-colour bitch Lassie was one of the early names to appear in the Smooth Collie awards.

Mr Megson had a great interest in Smooths as well as the Roughs, some of the Smooth Champions owned by him being Champion Melody, Champion Heatherfield Tip, Champion Heatherfield Nip, Champion Heatherfield Dot, Champion Heatherfield Biddy, Champion Beauty, Canute Wonder and Busy Bee. Champion Heatherfield Nip and Champion Heatherfield Tip were bred in August 1892 by Mr W. P. Phillips, by Jack Shepherd ex Ancrum Peeress. Heatherfield Tip and Heatherfield Gyp were the parents of Champion Gold Nugget, a Blue Merle who was bred by Mr J. Brown in March 1894. (This animal has been referred to as both a dog and a bitch. Unfortunately, being unable to find the registration, I cannot clarify this point, but I feel this dog must be mentioned, as it qualified as a Champion.)

Busy Bee and her brother Ballochmyle Max were home-bred, sired by Champion Heatherfield Tip, ex Champion Heatherfield Dot. Busy Bee later produced Champion Veto and Champion Village Girl, to Herdwick Smoker. (Herdwick Smoker was formerly known as Derby Smoker.) The sire of Herdwick Smoker was Derby Chieftain, owned by Mr A. Warde of Ormskirk. No information about this dog's breeding can be obtained.

Mr G. D. Paterson of Ancrum Bank, Lochee, Dundee, was the original owner of Ancrum Peeress. This bitch was a well-known winner, and her many wins included: 1st, Open Class, Dundee; 1st, Local Open Class, Dundee; 1st, Open Class, Glasgow K.C.; 1st, Open Class, Hamilton; 3rd, Open Class, Edinburgh; 2nd, Open Class, Crystal Palace, 1891; 3rd, Open Class, Cruft's 1892.

Ancrum Prioress was another bitch owned and bred by Mr Paterson in 1891. She was by Craigboy, ex Ancrum Ivy and was 3rd in the Open Class at Ayr in 1892.

Heatherfield Mac and Heatherfield Tyne were both winning dogs for Mr F. Hurst. Born on Christmas Day 1890, Mac, a Merle by Pickmere ex Lady Rosebery, won the Open Class, was 3rd, Novice and 2nd, Puppy Class, at Bakewell; 3rd, Open St Helens; 2nd, Open Hamilton; 3rd, Open Wigan; 1st, Open Crystal Palace; 3rd, Open Oldham; 1st, Open Birmingham. All these wins took place in 1891. After this: 1st, Open Manchester; 2nd, Open Class and Challenge Certificate at Islington. It appears from this and from other references that only one Challenge Certificate was offered at a particular show, unlike the present arrangement where two are offered, one for the dog and one for the bitch.

It is interesting to note that even in 1891 long distances were travelled to dog shows, before the convenience of cars.

In the early 1890s, the Heatherfield prefix was very much to the fore, Champion Heatherfield Dot having been placed first in the Open Classes at Cruft's and Manchester in 1891, and gaining a Challenge Certificate at Islington in 1892. Heatherfield Gyp also did her share of winning, one of the team to win the 'Cup Team Class' at Manchester in 1892, along with Champion Metchley Wonder, Edgbaston Fox, Matrimony, Westwood and Bagatelle. Heatherfield Kit (formerly known as Glen Ellen) was born in May 1890, sired by Wallace, ex Nellie (about whom no information has been obtained). She did a little winning for her owner Mr F. Hurst, along with Heatherfield Meg, who did her fair share of winning.

Heatherfield Pearl was owned by Mr A. J. Haskins of Bristol. This dog did well in the show ring: 1st, Open Class Southampton; 2nd, Open Class Leeds; 1st and Special, Open Class, Darlington; 1st, Open Class City of Liverpool; Challenge Certificate and 1st, Open Class Bishop Auckland 1891; 1st, Challenge Class Cruft's 1892.

For Mr Hastie and Mr Swinhoe, Herdwick Nell and Herdwick Princess, along with Herdwick Drover, Herdwick Hermit, Herdwick King and Herdwick Tudno, kept the flag flying.

Pickmere, the sire of Heatherfield Mac, was himself a well-known winner. He was owned by Mr A. D. Sutcliffe of Manchester and won the following prizes: 1st, Open Class Wakefield; 3rd, Open Class Bury; 1st, Challenge Class Darlington; 1st, Open Class Padiham; 1st, Open Class Darwen; 1st, Challenge Class Birmingham. All these awards were made in 1891. In 1892, he won: 1st, Challenge Class Liverpool; 1st, Challenge Class Manchester; 1st, Challenge Class and C.C. Islington.

Sefton Countess, who was owned by Mr J. Birch and Mr W. Birch, did her share of winning about the same time. Mr Walter Birch always had an eye for a Collie, be it Rough or Smooth, and was a most astute judge of both these coats. He was in partnership with his brother James in business as farmers and millers in Sefton, and also with the dogs. He was at one time Chairman of Wirral and Birkenhead Agricultural Society, Chairman of Sefton and District Council, and a County Justice of the Peace. In spite of all these commitments he was very interested in the dogs. Champion Sefton Grace and Champion Sefton Hero were two of the most famous dogs from this Kennel. It was reported that Mr Birch paid £250 for Hero as an unshown puppy. He was soon made a Champion and subsequently sold to Mr J. Pierpoint Morgan in the U.S.A.

Mr Birch was not only interested in Collies but also in fancy pigeons (in particular Jacobians) and poultry. He bred, exhibited and judged them. He supported his judgment by paying £25 (in 1909) for a Brahma Cock, and £40 for a Black Owl Cock. Such was his interest in all livestock.

During this period, Mr Robert Chapman of Glenboig, Scotland was a Smooth Collie Exhibitor. His Young Trim won one or two first prizes for his owner. Later on the prefix 'Heather' became very well known throughout the world for the outstanding Scottish Terriers bred at Glenboig; perhaps the most famous was that great dog Champion Heather Realisation.

Some Collies were registered without any information about their parents. One such entry was Lady Charles, born in April 1890. She was described as black-and-tan with white breast and feet. She was owned by Mr George Carter of Bedale, Yorkshire, who also owned her daughter Lady Christopher, sired by Pickmere Tom who was by Pickmere. With the progression of time, and with careful thought being given to pedigrees, some very nice Smooth Collies began to emerge. One of these was Champion Gold Nugget.

Bakewell Beauty was a bitch said to have been an asset to the breed. She was owned by Mr Smalley, and was by Veto ex Whitley Lass, bred by Mr J. Hough in 1897.

Mr Mumford Smith was one of the earliest of the Smooth exhibitors to establish a name, with his famous de Montforts. His interest in the Smooth Collie never faltered. As a girl, I remember going with my father to bring home a Tri-colour dog puppy from this world-famous kennel. The puppy was, if my memory serves me well, Chevalier de Montfort, a big fellow with wonderful bone, which was so characteristic of the stock from de Montfort. It was in 1899 that Mr Mumford Smith purchased, from Mr I. Smalley, Ashford Bluebell, by Ashford Royal ex Bakewell Beauty. This was the beginning of the kennel which had many famous champions to follow, including the Tri-colours, Champion Eleanor de Montfort and the lovely Champion Julien de Montfort. Champion Eleanor was born on 6 June 1903, by Count of Moreton ex Marston Amy; Champion Julien was born on 27 March 1907, by Champion Eastwood Eminent ex Genvia de Montfort. The latter was purchased by that other stalwart, Mr Frank Wildgoose, who had the Canute kennel. One of the early Smooth Canutes was Canute Fascination, bred by Mr Smalley in 1901, by Ashford Clinker ex Ashford Countess. Mr Smalley was very much in favour of Rough – Smooth mating. Ashford Royal was a Rough Collie, by Edgbaston Royal ex Curzon Blue Betty. Ashford Clinker was by Ashford Royal ex Bakewell Beauty.

Another well-known winner in the early part of the century was Champion Babette of Moreton, again a Tri-colour. She was bred by Mr A. Dunmore, whose Champion Irthlingboro' Village Lass, was born in 1898, by Irthlingboro' Village Boy ex Champion Village Girl.

Mr T. Stretch, so well known because of his many famous Ormskirk Roughs, owned a Champion Smooth, Ormskirk Venice, but he did not pursue this with the same vigour as Roughs. Venice was sired by Champion Barden Venture, ex Ormskirk Bluebelle, and most certainly did her fair share of winning, beating the Roughs when competing against them.

In 1902, Mr Farish bred a litter by the Rough Count of Moreton, ex Marston Amy. This mating was to produce the Smooth Champion Canute Perfection, who in turn was the sire of Champion Canute Model. Mr Wildgoose and the Canutes were responsible for producing some good stock, the lovely Champion Quality of Dunkirk being a daughter of Canute Fascination.

Quality of Dunkirk, in her turn, was the dam of Mr R. G. Howson's Champion Eastwood Eminent, who was sired by his owner's Champion

Sunnybrae Perfection. Other well-known winners from this kennel were Champion Eastwood Extra (who in his time won twenty-seven C.C.s, and was another product of a Rough-Smooth mating), Eastwood Exact, Stanley Wonder, and many others.

The mention of Stanley Wonder brings me to Mr G. Watson and the many Stanley Champions: Merle, Countess, and Elite (a Blue Merle who was purchased from Mr Swann, also a breeder of many good Smooths).

Champion Eastwood Eminent was the winner of twelve C.C.s before being exported to Mr Rutherford of Allamuchy, New Jersey, who at that time owned the top kennel of Smooth Collies in the United States of America. Mr Rutherford was also renowned for the famous team of Fox Terriers he owned.

Another good Smooth bitch was Connie of Dunkirk; she was a lovely Smooth Collie who made her presence felt, owned by Mr J. Radford, and by Eastwood Envoy ex Canute Fascination.

A retrospect by Mr Frank Wildgoose of the Smooth Collies shown during the year 1907 reads: 'The Smooth Collie of today is of far different type and quality than when I first entered the fancy twenty years ago and the competition now much keener. There is no denying the fact that the Smooth is making great headway, so much as that on several occasions they have competed against and defeated the Roughs in competition for premier honours. There are differences of opinion as to the correct type of a Smooth, but this should not be so, for every fancier should aim at, and ,carry out, the description and standard as laid down by the various Collie Clubs: the Smooth Collie differs from the rough only in its coat, which should be hard, dense and quite smooth. Doubts would then cease and snipey noses, weak muzzles and faulty mouths would soon be deleted.'

The opening and principal show of the year 1907 was held at Blackpool on 19 January under the auspices of the Northern Collie Club. A record entry was obtained for Roughs – the total entry being 590. Mr Wildgoose goes on to report that speaking from memory he held the record for Smooth entries. In 1895, when he was making his first appearance as a judge at the Liverpool Show, there was an entry of 92 Smooths in six classes; one class had 24 entries.

Just imagine what a wonderful sight these Smooths must have been. Can anyone explain why this cannot happen again, and the Smooth regain the popularity once enjoyed? By 1910 the Smooth entries were falling, and the various clubs were asking for private guarantees for the Smooth classes even though the Smooth Collie Club had recruited thirteen new members as against four the previous year – a total membership of 52 was recorded and Mr W. Baskerville, the Hon. Secretary, reported that the Club was in a satisfactory financial state.

Mr Baskerville was himself a successful breeder and exhibitor of both Rough and Smooth Collies. Champion Barden Venture was one of the Smooths to do his owner credit both in the ring and as a sire, even though his pedigree was unknown due to the fact that his previous owner had died when Venture was about seven months old, and the pedigree was never found. Mr Baskerville was the breed contributor for *Our Dogs*, and also the author of a book on Collies.

Mr Tom Harrison of Freshfield was a great handler of most dogs, but in particular the Collie. He handled dogs for many of the older breeders but in later years he became attached to Smooths and he had a most glorious champion Tri-colour bitch with whom he did a great deal of winning.

There were few changes in the early part of 1910. The winners of the Open Classes at the Northern Collie Club Show were as follows: *Dogs*: 1st, Stanley Wonder; 2nd, Stockport Bar None; 3rd, Canute Marvel. *Bitches*: 1st, Canute Quality; 2nd, Noreen de Montfort; 3rd, Canute Crystal.

At Birmingham the prizes awarded were: *Dogs*: 1st, Champion Stanley Wonder; 2nd, Canute Wonder; 3rd, Lucien de Montfort. *Bitches*: 1st, Stanley Jennie; 2nd, Canute Jennie; 3rd, Canute Constance.

At Cruft's: *Dogs*: 1st, Champion Stanley Wonder; 2nd, Canute Superior, *Bitches*: 1st, Champion Stockport Connie; 2nd, Colet Girl.

The Collie Club Show held 1 March: *Dogs*: 1st, Champion Julien de Montfort; 2nd, Eastwood Extra (who made his debut at this show); 3rd, Champion Stanley Wonder. *Bitches*: 1st, Champion Stockport Connie; 2nd, Champion Colet Lucy and 3rd, Canute Quality. One interesting feature of this show was that the Rough Champion Southport Sample took the Best in Show trophy for the fifth time.

Manchester again saw Julian and Extra heading off the opposition with Stockport Connie and Stanley Jennie doing likewise in bitches. Fourteen Smooth Collies were registered in January of that year, the Canutes, Stanleys and de Montforts having sired most of these. Stud fees were between one and two guineas.

Champion Eastwood Extra headed the dogs at Cruft's the following year. He was by Hector of Woolfold, ex Crosby Quality. The winning bitch was Eastwood Elda (by Marston Cyril ex Surprise).

The year 1911 saw Mr Herbert Harrison with a strong team of Smooths: Champion Julien de Montfort (by now the winner of sixteen Challenge Certificates), his son Canute Superior, and Canute Blue Boy.

The man in charge of this kennel was none other than the late Billie Dring, who used to be with the Primley Kennel and who later went to Mr T. H. Moorby of the Stainton Gundogs at Nelson, where he remained until the death of Mr Moorby and the subsequent disbanding of the kennel.

The report of the Smooth Collie Club for 1911 showed that the President's Cup had been won by Mr R. G. Howson's Champion Eastwood Extra who also won the Bendigo Cup. The Breeder's Dog Cup went to Mr A. Hastie's Herdwick Hermit and the Breeder's Bitch Cup to Mr J. Dunn's Butchers Lass. The club had as President, Mr A. Douthwaite. Messrs L. Cookson, R. G. Howson and G. Watson were Vice-Presidents. Mr Herbert Harrison was the Hon. Treasurer and of course, Mr Baskerville, Hon. Secretary.

Manchester that year showed the Smooths in favour again, an entry of 95 being recorded for the ten classes provided. Mr R. G. Howson was the judge and he awarded the championships to two puppies each of whom were being shown for the first time. The dog was Canute Premier, by Bennie ex Canute Queenie, owned by Mr Wildgoose. Canute Queenie was apparently one of those unlucky dogs we all have from time to time, or perhaps hear about. At the age of eight months she had a leg broken, spoiling her show career. It was decided to breed from her. Not long after she had been mated, she was run over, breaking another leg and receiving internal injuries. However, her puppies did not show any ill effects when they were born, and Premier must have been some consolation for her owner.

The other winning puppy was Stanley Countess, owned by Mr Watson by Champion Julien de Montfort ex Woodbine Fascination.

It was also reported at this time that several Smooths were exported to Germany, one such being Canute Julien (Champion Julien de Montfort ex Champion Stockport Connie).

1912 saw the puppy Canute Treasure taking the C.C. at the Northern Collie Club Show held on 18 January. This puppy was by Hector of Woolfold, ex Crosby Quality. Her elder brother, Champion Eastwood Extra, was Best Dog. This was also the order at Birmingham; Cruft's again saw Extra leading the dogs, but Treasure was beaten by Calderbank Countess, a daughter of Champion Eastwood Extra and Thorncliffe Irena, owned by Mr Harrison and handled by Billie Dring.

It was during this year that Mr Douthwaite tendered his resignation as President of the Smooth Collie Club and Mr H. Mumford Smith was elected in his place.

The Smooths continued their winning ways, and the lovely Canute Treasure became a Champion, on one occasion beating the great Eastwood Extra. The year following saw her daughter Canute Gem (by Canute Supreme) high in the awards, and the Primleys also coming to the fore.

At Bolton on New Year's Day 1914, Mr Arnold Clough showed

Canute Blue Belle; some of the older fanciers will remember with affection this loyal supporter of the Smooth Collie. He showed many, always good ones, but usually sold them before they gained their title. However, he did keep the last one he owned, nearly forty years later, to gain her title. This was Champion Peterblue Phillipa whom he made up and finally exported to Mrs J. Johnson of the United States in the 1950s. Though from time to time he exhibited other breeds with success, he always came back to the Collie. It was a sad day for me when, in February 1970, I attended Arnold Clough's cremation; he is sadly missed by his many Collie friends.

At Manchester in 1914, the Smooths were described as the best seen for some time and averaged seven per class. Champion Eastwood Extra again won the Special for Best Rough or Smooth. At this show, Leyland Lucifer (owned by the Threlfall Brothers) made his appearance, and was runner up to Extra in his class. Many more Leylands were to follow, bringing success to their owners.

The Club reported a substantial profit and an increase in membership; this picture was typical as time went by. The Smooth fanciers were keeping the type and quality. More fanciers took up the interest, amongst which came Mr Anderson and the Saltaires, and Mr W. W. Stansfield with the Launds. One of the first Smooths to join this latter kennel was Torside Lady.

All these fanciers did a great deal for the breed, and consistently bred Champions.

My earliest recollection of any dog is of Champion Laund Lynne, born on 6 September 1917, by Hetman ex Primley Primula. She was my father's constant companion and lived in the house. She would round up the sheep or fetch in the cattle and was often to be seen walking the hedges and retrieving a rabbit which my father had shot. You might think that this versatile dog was just a pet, but she was the winner of sixteen Challenge Certificates and 291 first prizes, and was placed 95 times as Best in Show All Breeds or Best Bitch in Show; in one year, she annexed the Cup for Best in Show All Breeds at the English Kennel Club Show, at the Birmingham Show, and at the Scottish Kennel Club Show. She also won outright the Silver Jardiniére of the English Kennel Club Show, taking the award for Best Bitch in Show All Breeds three years running. Not having much time to rear puppies during her show days, at ten years of age she reared a litter of seven puppies. This beautiful Blue Merle bitch was bred by Mr Whitley of Paignton who at that time owned privately the Zoo at Paignton, and who specialised in producing 'blue' in all forms of animal life.

It has always been a Smooth Collie who has guarded our house, and I cannot quite imagine living without a Smooth Collie. Champion

Laund Lawson was born on 14 December 1929, took over from Champion Laund Lynne, and was my constant companion. Perhaps you will understand how devoted he was when I tell you that he fretted after the birth of my son, possibly feeling that he was no longer receiving all my attention; there was nothing we could do to pacify him, and so I lost one of my dearest pals. Another instance of the devotion received from a Smooth Collie was that of Champion Laund Lanry (son of Champion Laund Lawson) who was sold to Mrs Pleydell-Bouverie, yet who never forgot me. Many of the older fanciers will remember that even after he left Laund, he was usually handled at the shows by us. He eventually came back when the war started, as he had never really settled in his new home. From then onwards he was my constant companion until his death.

Champion Laund Lawson (born 14 December 1929). Owner Mr W. W. Stansfield. By Laund Blue Charmer ex Laund Lya

Many of our Smooth Collie puppies who did not quite make the grade were sent to farmers in the neighbouring districts; they were easily trained to work both cattle and sheep, thereby proving the versatility of the breed both as a show dog and as a worker. In addition to the Collie being a worker, the following is an example of how the Smooth has the ability of being a gun dog. Mrs Newman, who exhibited Smooth Collies before World War II, had two dogs Cereula and Ruin. These dogs were used by her husband as gun dogs, and Mr Newman declared that his invitation to attend shooting parties increased considerably when it was found what a wonderful gun dog the Smooth Collie was. In addition to the two Smooths mentioned, Laund Lawgirl was also used for this purpose. Another dog owned by Mrs Newman was Laund Linteria, a Challenge Certificate winner whose show career was cut short by World War II.

Between the wars, the Smooth flag was kept flying by such experienced breeders as Mr Bart Hewison, whose Hewburns were well known for their wonderful type. In fact, round the Northumberland and Durham area, Smooth Collies were very popular, with Mr Alec Hastie (Herdwick) and his friend Mr Watson maintaining the old strains. Around the Manchester area too, the Smooth Collies were popular, with Mr Arthur Newton and his famous Champion Gypsy Meg, Mr Wilf Schofield and his Marwins, and his daughter, Mrs Mary Sawdon, who still has more than a passing interest in the breed.

We are fortunate that Mrs Z. M. Rhys still maintains a lively interest in Smooth Collies and the Smooth Collie Club of Great Britain, her Hughleys being one of the few names to be known both before and after World War II. The most recent winner to carry the affix is Champion Blue Heritage at Hughley, who took the Best in Show award at the British Collie Club Show in 1976.

The late Miss E. Dundas-Mouat with eight Peterblue Champions.

Mr Herbert Farrington too, was one of the old stalwarts. This famous Wythenshawe prefix has been known for many years. His daughter often accompanied her father to the shows, and perhaps one day we shall see Mrs Zonic resume her interest in the Breed.

Champion Copster Treasure owned by Mrs Wade was a truly beautiful Tri-colour bitch; her constant battles in the ring with the lovely Champion Rosaleen, owned by Miss Sumner, were legion.

It was not until after World War II that Miss Elizabeth Dundas-Mouat and her partner Mrs K. Alexander took an interest in the Smooth Collie. The purchase of Champion Redevalley Rosita of Ladypark was the start of the now famous Peterblues, most of whom originally came from this beautiful bitch and her liaison with Rough Collie dogs.

One dog to emerge from this kennel was International Ch. Peterblue Harvey, owned by Miss M. Meyer in Switzerland. Not only was he an International Champion, but he also held a Gold Medal for his work as a 'Sanitary Dog'. The word 'Sanitary' in this context probably gives a wrong impression; in English the name is better defined 'rescue'.

FIGURE 11:
International Champion
Peterblue Harvey.

These dogs are trained to search for injured or lost people, and they can cover large areas in mountainous country. They do not work specifically on a scent, but on a more random basis, finding lost and injured persons. These Rescue Dogs wear a small jacket on which is printed the Red Cross, which obviates the danger of the dogs being shot or molested in any way. Round his neck the dog wears a collar to which is attached, at the front beneath his chin, a chain, to which is fastened a leather cigar-shaped pendant about six inches long. This pendant, known as a 'temoin', is used to show when the dog has found his quarry. He takes it in his mouth, and does not drop the pendant until he is ordered, carrying it from the accident area until he reaches his handler. The handler then attaches a lead to the dog and is led to the injured or lost person.

The training for this work is quite rigorous and includes obedience training, guarding, swimming, jumping over obstacles, etc. In Switzerland, the dog licence fee is very high, but dogs engaged in this work are given a fifty per cent concession. The dogs, however, are liable to be called upon at any time by the authorities if they are required for work.

International Champion Peterblue Harvey was a Class III Sanitary Dog, the highest grade to be granted. (I thank Miss M. Meyer for supplying this information.)

Left: Champion Cotsbelle Blue Caprice. Owner Mrs K. Alexander. By Gorjess Black Arab ex Ch. Peterblue Love in a Mist. Breeder Mrs B. Hodgetts.

Right: Champion Peterblue Chrystobel (owner and breeder Mrs K. Alexander; by Peterblue Zebadee ex Peterblue Periwinkle), Champion Cotsbelle Blue Caprice and Champion Cotsbelle Blue Finesse (owner Mrs K. Alexander; by Gorjess Black Arab ex Ch. Peterblue Love in a Mist; breeder Mrs B. Hodgetts).

This dog, you remember, is from Mrs Alexander's kennel. It was, I believe, in the late 1940s that she began to show her Rough Collie dog, a Blue Merle called Merrion Blue Peter. Following the purchase of Ch. Redevalley Rosita of Ladypark with Miss Dundas-Mouat, several attempts to breed from this bitch were made. After some failures, this daughter of Champion Grangetown Blue Prince and Redevalley Roseline, bred by the Foster brothers, produced some very fine puppies from the mating to Merrion Blue Peter (by Group Captain, ex Merrion Sequence). From these puppies, six Champions resulted. She produced, amongst others, Peterblue Martie (the dam of Champion Peterblue Sophie), and to Hewburn Liquorice of Ladypark, Peterblue Callum (Sophie's sire). Thus began the era of Peterblue and of the many Champions who followed. Mrs Joan Hill had the beautiful Champion Selskars Peterblue Susan and, of course, many Selskars to make the name famous.

Miss J. Stewart, the owner of the Foxtwichen Kennel, was at one time the Secretary of the Smooth Collie Club of Great Britain. Mr

Purvis, so well known in Rough Collies, owned the Smooth Champion Danvis Blue Prince. Another lovely Blue Merle was Champion Krystal of Rodlea, owned by the late Mrs Nan Leach. We now have another Mrs Leach, not related to Nan: Mrs Christine Leach. She was the owner of Champion Selskars Blue Tarn, and breeder of Mrs Rhys's Champion Blue Heritage at Hughley. Mrs Leach imported his dam, Kelbounnie Chan-El Gina, who was in whelp to American Champion Golrath O'Darjoro. Blue Heritage was probably the best-known winner from the litter. Mrs Leach took over from Miss Stewart as Club Secretary of the Smooth Collie Club.

There are several new names in the Smooth Collie pages of the Show Catalogues, but some that sadly are gone forever. John Liversidge, well known as the owner of, amongst other Smooths, Champion Peterblue Nigel, Champion Jalondas Petronella, and Champion Jalondas Marie Theresa, was the victim of a fatal car crash; the kennel was disbanded.

Mrs M. Byrnes is no longer exhibiting her Smooths in this country, having now gone to live in West Germany. Once again the Smooth Collie Club lost its Secretary, since Mrs Byrnes had taken over from Mrs Leach. However, it was Mrs Byrnes who was able to announce that the Smooth Collie Club of Great Britain had been granted Challenge Certificates for Smooth Collies at its Show to be held in 1979. It was Mrs Bratley, then Secretary, who did most of the work for that memorable show.

Mrs Iris Combe, another Rough Collie enthusiast, is the owner of Champion Tilehouse Patrick, winner of 20 C.C.s (a post-war record); 19 of these were won under different judges, and on three occasions he was the Best Smooth Dog at Cruft's.

Champion Tilehouse Patrick (born 26 June 1971). Breeder and owner Mrs I. Combe. By Ch. Selskars Blue Tarn ex Robec Ramona.

Centre: International Champion (Norwegian and English) Foxearth Silver Fountain (born 27 May 1973). Breeders and owners Mr and Mrs T. Hayward. By Ch. Wingbelle Lian ex Australian Ch. Foxearth Black Faith.

Below left: Champion Foxearth Jubilant (born 20 May 1977). Breeder Mr T. Hayward. By Ch. Blue Heritage at Hughley ex Ch. Jalondas Jacanapes. Owners Mr and Mrs G. C. Duffield.

Below right: Champion Chicnoir Midnight Sultan (born 20 December 1974). Breeder Miss P. Hindes. By Crossfells Sea Tanden ex Dancerwood Diamond Lil. Owners Mr and Mrs M. W. Marsh.

Not very long ago, there were few Sable-and-Whites being shown: Mrs Taylor had Crossfells Champions in this colour, and Mrs White has Champion Dancerwood Freelance.

It is refreshing to see a number of young people now showing; we hope that the breed may gain popularity through their efforts.

To mention just a few of the devotees, one thinks of Mrs Cornish, Mr and Mrs Trundley, Mr and Mrs Clarke, Mrs Lister, Mrs Hardy, Mr and Mrs Marsh and, of course, Mr and Mrs Duffield, who have been doing well with their Champion Foxearth Jubilant, bred by Mr Trevor Hayward (by Champion Blue Heritage at Hughley, ex Champion Jalondas Jacanapes). Champion Foxearth Jubilant is (at mid-1979) winner of 5 C.C.s, four with Best of Breed, and three Reserve C.C.s. In 1979 she was Best of Breed at Cruft's and a finalist in the Working Group. In 1978 she won all the Smooth Collie Points Trophies. She was unbeaten at Open Shows in her Breed Classes, had one Best in Show win, and was the Reserve Best in Show twice, and also Best Oppositie Sex twice; she won the Working Group four times. She also had the honour of being the Best Unclassified Puppy eight times, Reserve for Best Puppy, three, and was Best Unclassified eight times, including the Peterborough Championship Show. All this, too, occurred when she was just over two years old. Perhaps we shall again see Smooths taking top honours at the Championship Shows. Mr and Mrs Marsh have won 12 Certificates with Champion Chicnoir Midnight Sultan, and are to be seen at most of the Championship Shows.

It will be noticed from the breeding details I have given in this chapter that most of the leading winners from the very earliest days until recently have had the Rough – Smooth cross playing an extremely important part. The inter-breeding of Rough and Smooth Collies is now only possible by the special permission of the Kennel Club, however.

The Standard of the Collie (Smooth)

Characteristics. To enable the Collie to fulfil a natural bent for sheepdog work, its physical structure should be on the lines of strength and activity, free from cloddiness and without any trace of coarseness. Expression, one of the most important points in considering relative values, is obtained by the perfect balance and combination of skull and foreface, size, shape, colour and placement of eye, correct position and carriage of ears. Temperament should be gay and friendly, never nervous nor aggressive.

General appearance. The Collie should instantly appear as gifted with intelligence, alertness and activity. He should stand with dignity, and his movements, governed by perfect anatomical formation, with no part out of proportion, should be smooth and graceful. He should give the appearance of a dog capable of working.

Head and skull. The head properties are of great importance and must be considered in proportion to the size of the dog. When viewed from both front and profile the head should bear a general resemblance to a well-blunted, clean wedge, being smooth in outline. The skull should be flat. The sides should taper gradually and smoothly from the ears to the end of the black nose, without prominent cheek bones or pinched muzzle. Viewed in profile, the top of the skull and the top of the muzzle should lie in two parallel, straight planes of equal length, divided by a slight but perceptible 'stop' or break. A mid-point between the inside corners of the eyes (which is the centre of a correctly placed 'stop') should be the centre of balance in length of head. The end of the smooth, well-rounded muzzle should be blunt, but not square. The underjaw should be strong, clean cut, and the depth of the skull from the brow to the underpart of the jaw should never be excessive (deep through). Whatever the colour of the dog, the nose must be black.

Eyes. A very important feature, which should give a sweet expression to the dog. They should be of medium size, set somewhat obliquely, of almond shape and of dark brown colour, except in the case of Blue Merles when one or both eyes may be wall or jewelled. Expression: full of intelligence with a quick, alert look when listening.

Ears. Should be moderately large, wider at the base, and placed not too close together nor too much on the side of the head. When in repose they should be carried thrown back, but when on the alert brought forward and carried semi-erect, that is, with approximately two-thirds of the ear standing erect, the top third tipping forward naturally, below the horizontal.

Mouth. The teeth should be of good size, with the lower incisors fitting closely behind the upper incisors; a very slight space is not to be regarded as a serious fault.

Neck. Should be muscular, powerful, of fair length and well arched.

Forequarters. The shoulders should be sloped and well angulated. The forelegs should be straight and muscular, neither in nor out at the elbows, with a moderate amount of bone. The forearm somewhat fleshy with pasterns showing flexibility without weakness.

Body. Should be a trifle long compared with the height, back level and firm with a slight rise over the loins; ribs well-sprung; chest deep and fairly broad behind the shoulders.

Hind-quarters. The hind legs should be muscular at the thighs, clean and sinewy below, with well bent stifles. Hocks well let-down and powerful. Male animals should have two apparently normal testicles fully descended into the scrotum.

Feet. Should be oval with soles well padded. Toes arched and close together. Hind feet slightly less arched.

Gait. Movement is a distinct characteristic of the breed. A sound dog is never out at elbow, yet it moves with its front feet comparatively close together. Plaiting, crossing or rolling are highly undesirable. The hind legs, from the hock joint to the ground, when viewed from the rear, should be parallel, powerful and full of drive. Viewed from the side the action should be smooth. A reasonably long stride is desirable and this should be light and appear quite effortless.

Tail. Should be long, with the bone reaching at least to the hock joint. To be carried low when the dog is quiet but with a slight upward swirl at the tip. It may be carried gaily when the dog is excited, but never over the back.

Coat. A very important feature of the Smooth Collie is his short, flat top coat of harsh texture, with a very dense undercoat.

Colour. The three recognised colours are: Sable-and-White, Tri-colour and Blue Merle.

Sable: Any shade from light gold to rich mahogany or shaded sable. Light straw or cream colour is highly undesirable.

Tri-colour: Predominantly black with rich tan markings about the legs and head. A rusty tinge in the top coat is highly undesirable.

Blue Merle: Predominantly clear, silvery blue, splashed and marbled with black. Rich tan markings to be preferred, but their absence should not be counted as a fault. Large black markings, slate colour or a rusty tinge on the top of undercoat are highly undesirable.

White markings: All the above colours may carry the typical white Collie markings to a greater or lesser degree. The following markings are favourable: white collar, full or part; white front legs and feet; white tail tip. A blaze may be carried on muzzle or skull or both. All white or predominantly white is most undesirable.

Weight and Size. Dogs: 22–24 in. at shoulder. Bitches: 20–22 in. at shoulder. Dogs: 45–65 lb. Bitches: 40–55 lb.

Faults. Any departure from the foregoing points should be considered a fault, and the seriousness of the fault should be in exact proportion to its degree.

13 The Bearded Collie

Having searched for the history of the Bearded Collie without a great deal of success, my findings being somewhat meagre, I came upon an article written by J. Russell Greig, M.R.C.V.S. in January 1913 for the *Collie Folio*. The gentleman obviously knew a great deal more than most people about the Bearded Collie and his origin and the following article gives what I consider to be a very likely concept of the beginning of the Beardie.

FIGURE 12:
Artist's impression of Bearded Collie: The Laird of Dumbiedykes (owned by J. Russell Greig, M.R.C.V.S.)

THE BEARDED COLLIE by J. Russell Greig M.R.C.V.S.
'A big rough "tousy" looking tyke with a coat not unlike a doormat, the texture of the hair hard and fibry and the ears hanging close to the head.'

Such is the description of the Scottish Bearded Collie given by the author of *Dogs of Scotland*.

It is a description in which one can find little amiss, for a 'tyke' – in the general acceptance of the term – he assuredly is.

He has none of the polish and noblesse of his English cousin, the Bobtail, but there is a rough rugged grandeur about him, which is wholly in keeping with his natural surroundings – his native hills.

His being essentially a worker, however, does not preclude his boasting an ancient lineage, but to trace his origin is no mean task.

Had the 'Beardie', like the Bloodhound and Greyhound, been owned in olden times by the noblemen and gentlemen of the country, records of his ancestry and history would have been more numerous but his deeds have not been emblazoned in the records of the trail and the chase. He is, and has always been, a hill herd's dog – a humble worker.

Few dogs, except those used for hunting, were thought worthy of notice in days gone by, and the dog's origin, as a consequence, is 'wrapt in the dim obscurity of buried centuries'.

Our knowledge of the history of the British Sheepdog is, as has been indicated, extremely meagre, but is nevertheless interesting, and carries us back to earliest times.

The great biologist Buffon held that the Sheepdog was the source of all our other breeds. How far this is true is an open question.

The fact that sheep raising is one of the oldest occupations would seem to lend support to such a contention, for it would not be long before the domesticated dog would be recognised as a valuable assistant to the shepherd.

So far as our knowledge goes, it is to the Welsh King Howel Dda, who reigned early in the tenth century, that we are indebted for the first reference to the Sheepdog in Britain, for in a code of laws he personally drew up, and in that part which refers to the worth of dogs, appears the following:

'18 Whosoever possesses a cur, though it be the King, its value is fourpence.

'19 A herd dog that goes before the herd in the morning and follows them home at night is worth the best ox.' [Dalziel]

What the actual appearance of the ancient British Sheepdog was, we have little idea. Appian's description of the dog used by the ancient Caledonians is crude, and though it would appear to be some sort of hunting terrier, no definite conclusion can be arrived at.

Dr Johannes Caius, writing in the sixteenth century, minutely describes the work of the Sheepdog, but unfortunately omits to give any more than a very vague description of the dog itself. One has frequently heard it supposed that the bearded Collie is of comparatively recent origin, and indeed so great an authority as Hugh Dalziel suggested that he was a cross between the Collie and the Old English Sheepdog. Still there are many others who believed the Bearded Collie to be one of the most ancient breeds in these Islands, a contention which it is the author's purpose to forward.

There are two lines of evidence which support this claim – one is furnished by the dog's natural history, the other by his racial history.

Take them in turn. It is one of the most salient characteristics of the dog that he breeds 'true to type'; no matter what crosses are introduced; the typical 'Beardie' characters are predominant, and are indelibly stamped upon the offspring. This is surely not what one would expect in a recent, adventitiously manufactured breed – the result of a first cross – and one would instance it as a proof of his antiquity and concentration of strain.

As has been stated above, the Bobtail is by some regarded as a possible progenitor of the 'Beardie'.

One is firmly convinced, however, that the relationship which exists between the two breeds could be better likened to that of cousins – i.e. they are both descendants from a common stock.

The likeness between the two breeds is remarkable, but it is still more remarkable when one compares the working English Sheepdog and the 'Beardie', for we must remember that the former has been much improved since the formation of the Old English Sheepdog Club.

The author has in his possession a sketch made about twenty years ago of Mr Weager's Grizzle Bob and Dairy Maid – Bobtails, which, although considered among the best specimens of their time, bear a strong resemblance to the 'Beardie' rather than to their successors on the show bench today.

The most noticeable difference between the two breeds is, of course, the absence in the Bobtail of a caudal appendage. We know, however, that this is not an infallible characteristic of the breed, and that many a Sheepdog puppy acquires his 'bob' by means of the docking knife.

Philip Reinagle's historic picture of 'The Sheepdog', one of a series of paintings, which was reproduced in the *Sportsman's Cabinet* (1804) is of peculiar interest in this respect. Here we have a presumably typical Old English Sheepdog with quite a respectable tail, which, if shown to a Scottish shepherd today, would be pronounced a Bearded Collie. Further, in the text we are told that 'the breed is propagated and preserved with the greatest respect to purity in the northern parts of the kingdom as well as in the highlands of Scotland.'

Gordon James Phillips, of Glenlivet, in a letter which appeared in the 'Live Stock Journal' for 15 November 1878, speaks of a strain of the Bearded Collie with a tail which he describes as 'simply a stump, generally from six to nine inches in length'. Whether this was a true 'Beardie' indigenous to the district, or merely the imported English Bobtail, one is unable to learn.

When discussing the origin of the Collie, Dalziel remarked: 'I think it not improbable that the Scotch Collie may in part be derived from the English form of Sheepdog and the Scotch Greyhound.' But in consideration of the undoubted antiquity of the Bearded Collie, one is led to agree with Gray, and consider it just as probable that the Scotch Collie may be derived in part from the Scotch form of Sheepdog and the Scotch Greyhound.

When we come to consider the Continental breeds of Sheepdog we are again struck by their resemblance to our Bobtail and Beardie.

The French Chien de Berger de la Brie, were it not for his semi-prick ears, might pass for a little brother of the Bearded Collie, while the Owtchar, found along the banks of the Dneiper, is his Russian prototype.

Indeed, so striking is the family resemblance in the Sheepdog, that one is led to believe they have all a common stock and are merely the branches of the same family tree.

Assuming this to be correct, it is possible that the British Sheepdog was imported into this country at a very early date and may possibly have a Gallic origin.

It is only within the last few days that the Bearded Collie Club has been formed in Edinburgh, under the presidency of Mr Jas. C. Dalgliesh.

At the present moment the breed is not recognised by the Kennel Club, and it is hoped that one of the first actions of the new club will be to appeal to the proper authorities to set this matter to rights. The primary object of the club is to preserve the breed, and it has many claims for support.

The dog has been the mainstay of many generations of flockmasters, and having been exclusively bred for brains and stamina, he has an intelligence and constitution equalled by few.

The club Standard is presently being compiled, and one shall not venture to go into a minute description of his 'points', but it is resolved to keep the dog as much as possible in the state in which he exists throughout Scotland today, and at all costs let him remain a worker.

One might fittingly conclude this short article on the Bearded Collie with the following quotation from Alfred Olliphant's *Owd Bob*.

'Should you, while wandering in the wild sheep land, happen on moor or in market upon a very perfect gentle knight, clothed in dark grey habit, splashed here and there with rays of moon; free by right divine of the guild of gentlemen, strenuous as a prince, lithe as a rowan, graceful as a girl, with high king carriage, motions and manners of a fairy queen, should he have a noble breadth of brow, an air of still strength born of right confidence, all unassuming; last and most unfailing test of all, should you look into two snowclad eyes, calm, wistful inscrutable, their soft depths clothed on with eternal sadness – yearning, as is said, for the soul that is not theirs –know then, that you look upon one of the line of the most illustrious Sheepdogs of the North.'

The Kennel

It is worthy of note that although the first Bearded Collie Club was formed in 1913, the breed was not considered by the Kennel Club to be worthy of having Challenge Certificates granted until 1959.

It is also interesting to note that several characteristics of the Beardie are at variance with those of the other two varieties of Collie. Since all these dogs were produced to do the same kind of work, this does seem to be remarkable.

The Bearded Collie bears little resemblance to the Rough and the Smooth Collie and does not enjoy the popularity of the Rough Collie. Whilst I do not own any Bearded Collies, I do not consider that any book which bears the title *All about the Collie* would be complete without some reference to the 'Beardie', even though there is now a companion volume in this series about the breed.

The Kennel Club did not grant certificates for Bearded Collies until 1959 when certificates were awarded at Cruft's. The first Champion Bearded Collie was Champion Beauty Queen of Bothkennar, owned by Mrs. G. O. Willison. The breed owes much to her as she was responsible for breeding many well-known 'Beardies', the Bothkennars are predominant in most of today's pedigrees.

Champion Wishanger Barley of Bothkennar was the first Champion dog. He was owned by Miss M. Partridge and was a slate-white. Up to 1970, only 25 Champions had been made; included in this number were the brother and sister Champion Osmart Bonnie Blue Braid and Champion Osmart Bonnie Black Pearl. They were bred by Mr and Mrs K. Osborne, by Champion Bravo of Bothkennar ex Champion Blue Bonnie of Bothkennar. Mr and Mrs Osborne owned Champion Osmart Black Pearl and their daughter Catherine, Champion Osmart Blue Braid. Miss S. J. Holmes's Ch. Bracken Boy of Bothkennar was bred by Mrs Willison by Ch. Bravo of Bothkennar out of Ch. Blue Bonnie of Bothkennar.

All the above-mentioned are grandchildren of Ch. Beauty Queen of Bothkennar, and it can be seen from the above breeding just how much the stock from Mrs Willison's famous kennel has meant to Beardies. Mrs Willison must surely be missed by the Beardie fraternity, her experience and knowledge being so vast. Stock carrying Bothkennar bloodlines continues the tradition started by this respected lady.

During recent years Beardies have become more popular, perhaps because they have made their presence felt in the 'Big Ring'. The first to win a Group was Mr A. Drake's Ch. Andrake Persephone (by Ch. Davealex Royale Brigadier ex Osmart Black Beth); her Group win at

Champion Osmart Bonnie Blue Braid. Owner Miss C. Osborne. Bred by Mr and Mrs K. Osborne. By Ch. Bravo of Bothkennar ex Ch. Blue Bonnie of Bothkennar.

Blackpool was a great thrill. Persephone is the winner of 16 C.C.s, 13 Reserve C.C.s and 8 Best of Breeds. History had been made, but there was more to come. Miss S. J. Holmes was to achieve the highest honours with Ch. Edenborough Blue Bracken, home-bred by Rowdina Grey Fella ex Blue Maggie from Osmart. He was born on 1 March 1970. Blue Bracken was the first Bearded Collie to win Supreme Best in Show at a Championship Show. In England he was Best in Show at Windsor, at the Working Breeds Championship Show, and at the Midland Counties Championship Show. He is the winner of 39 C.C.s – a breed record – including twice Best of Breed at Cruft's. He has also made several trips to Ireland, winning Reserve Best in Show at the Irish Kennel Club Championship Show, Best in Show at Limerick Championship Show, Best in Show at the Combined Canine Championship Show, Reserve Best in Show at Kilkenney, and twice the Working Group. He was Reserve Best in Show at Tralee Championship Show on two occasions, and in 1979 Blue Bracken won the first

Green Star awarded in Breed Classes in Ireland. He won also the Pedigree Petfoods 'Veteran of the Year' in 1978. Not only was he a 'top dog' in the ring, but he was the sire of 32 Champions both in the United Kingdom and abroad.

Champion Andrake Persephone (born 9 March 1972). Breeder and owner Mr A. Drake. By Ch. Davealex Royale Brigadier ex Osmart Black Beth.

Bearded Collies seem to be good at record-breaking. Mr and Mrs Forrest, who live in Renfrewshire, bought a Beardie and decided to show her. Imagine their delight when Robday Wild Affair not only won the C.C., but also the Working Group and Reserve Best in Show at Kelso. Doubtless more Beardies will join the family.

Another who has kept in the public eye is Ch. Pepperland Lyric John at Potterdale. He is owned by Mr and Mrs Lewis, and is by Wishanger Butter Tubs Pass by Quinbury ex Pepperland Pandamonium. At Birmingham in 1978, he won his 14th C.C., at the age of 3 years 5 months. He was also Reserve in the Group.

It is apparent that the Bearded Collie can hold its own with any breed. If you require any further information about them I suggest you contact the Secretary of your nearest Club.

Bearded Collie Club of Great Britain. Mrs M. Reader, 1 Woden Road South, Golf Links Estate, Wednesbury, West Midlands.

Southern Counties Bearded Collie Club. Mrs B. White, 107 Janson Road, Shirley, Southampton.

Bearded Collie Club of Scotland. Mrs M. McVake, Middlefield, 9 Kirkintilloch Road, Lenzie, Kirkintilloch.

The Standard of the Bearded Collie.

Characteristics. The Bearded Collie must be alert, and should be lively, self-confident and active. The temperament should be that of a steady intelligent working dog, with no signs of nervousness or aggression.

General appearance. A lean active dog, longer than it is high in an approximate proportion of 5 to 4, measured from point of chest to point of buttock. Bitches may be slightly longer. The breed, though strongly made, should show plenty of daylight under the body and should not look too heavy. A bright, enquiring expression is a distinctive feature of the breed.

Head and skull. The head should be in proportion to the size of the dog. The skull broad and flat and square, the distance between stop

Left: Champion Edenborough Blue Bracken (born 1 March 1970). Breeder and owner Miss S. J. Holmes. By Rowdina Grey Fella ex Blue Maggie from Osmart.

Right: Champion Pepperland Lyric John at Potterdale (born 11 May 1975). Breeder Ms Samuels. By Wishanger Butter Tubs Pass By Quinbury ex Pepperland Pandamonium. Owners Mr and Mrs M. Lewis.

and occiput being equal to the width between the orifices of the ears. The muzzle strong and equal in length to the distance between the stop and the occiput, the whole effect being that of a dog with strength of muzzle and plenty of brain room. The stop should be moderate. The nose large and square, generally black but normally following the coat colour in blues and browns. The nose and lips should be of solid colour without spots or patches. Pigmentation of lips and eye rims should follow nose colour.

Eyes. The eyes should tone with coat in colour, be set widely apart and be large, soft and affectionate, but not protruding. The eyebrows arched up and forward but not so long as to obscure the eyes.

Ears. The ears of medium size and drooping. When the dog is alert, the ears should lift at the base level with, but not above, the top of the skull, increasing the apparent breadth of the skull.

Mouth. The teeth large and white, the incisors of the lower jaw fitting tightly behind those of the upper jaw. However, a pincer bite is acceptable.

Neck. Moderate length, muscular and slightly arched.

Forequarters. The shoulders should slope well back: a line drawn through the centre of the shoulder blade should form a right angle (90°) with the humerus. The shoulder blades at the withers should be separated only by the vertebrae, but should slope outwards from there sufficiently to accommodate the desired spring of rib. Legs straight and vertical, with good bone, and covered with shaggy hair all round. Pasterns flexible without weakness.

Body. The length of the back should come from the length of the ribcage and not that of the loin. The back level and ribs well sprung but not barrelled. The loins should be strong and the chest deep, giving plenty of heart and lung room.

Hind-quarters. Well muscled with good second thighs, well bent stifles and low hocks. The lower leg should fall at a right angle to the ground and, in normal stance, should be just behind a line vertically below the point of the buttock.

Feet. Oval in shape with the soles well padded. The toes arched and close together, well covered with hair including between the pads.

Gait. Movement should be supple, smooth and long reaching, covering the ground with the minimum of effort.

Tail. Set low, without kink or twist, and long enough for the end of the bone to reach at least the point of the hock. Carried low with an upward swirl at the tip whilst standing or walking, but may be extended at speed. Never carried over the back. Covered with abundant hair.

Coat. Double with the undercoat soft, furry and close. Outercoat flat, harsh, strong and shaggy, free from woolliness and curl, though a slight wave is permissible. Length and density of the hair should be sufficient to provide a protective coat and to enhance the shape of the dog, but not enough to obscure the natural lines of the body. The coat must not be trimmed in any way. On the head, the bridge of the nose should be sparsely covered with hair which is slightly longer on the side just to cover the lips. From the cheeks, the lower lips and under the chin, the coat should increase in length towards the chest, forming the typical beard.

Colour. Slate grey, reddish fawn, black, blue, all shades of grey, brown and sandy, with or without white markings. Where white occurs it should appear on the foreface, as a blaze on the skull, on the tip of the tail, on the chest, legs and feet and, if round the collar, the roots of the white hair should not extend behind the shoulder. White should not appear above the hocks on the outside of the hind legs. Slight tan markings are acceptable on the eyebrows, inside the ears, on the cheeks, under the root of the tail, and on the legs where white joins the main colour.

Size. Ideal height at the shoulder: Dogs: 53–56 cm (21–22 in.). Bitches: 51–53 cm (20–21 in.). Overall quality and proportions should be considered before size, but excessive variation from the ideal height should be discouraged.

Faults. Any departure from the foregoing points should be considered a fault, and the seriousness with which the fault is regarded should be in exact proportion to its degree.

Note: Male animals should have two apparently normal testicles fully descended into the scrotum.

14   The Launds

Most people can tell you how and when they first became interested in the Collie. Perhaps it was the Collie films about 'Lassie' – incidentally at this point, we may mention that Lassie was not a Lassie at all, but a Laddie! Perhaps they visited a dog show and saw a Collie, maybe a Rough Collie with his glorious coat (surely one of the most attractive features, along with his beautiful head which even to the very beginners must have an enormous appeal). From his intelligent eye, one gets that characteristic look which I do not think any other breed of dogs can quite give – are we suggesting a game or a walk? In short, the Collie is an animal – whatever the variety may be – who is certain to give a great deal of pleasure to his owner.

In my particular case, I was just adopted by the Collies, who were there before I was. I grew up with those magnificent dogs around me.

I have been asked from time to time how the Launds first began; I will tell you. It was much the usual story – my mother bought a Collie bitch as a present for my father, purely as a pet. Being the sort of man that he was, my father considered that this was not quite good enough and soon there were more Collies, the prefix 'Laund' really becoming known before World War 1. As I have said earlier, Ch. Laund Limit was the first Champion. Up to 1948 the total number of Champions owned by my late father was fifty-nine. Rough and Smooth Collies both played their part, and like me, I do not think my father had any preference. It is from the original owner of Laund, Mr Ainscough, and Mr T. H. Stretch, that I learnt the little bit I know about the Collie. I do not think that one ever finishes one's education on this subject.

To say which would be the best of the great number of Champions would be an extremely difficult task and one that I would not be prepared to undertake. I suggest that Lynne must rank very high on the list and I know that International Champion Laund Lero was one of my father's favourites.

The year 1924 was the year in which the Launds won the four certificates at Birmingham National Show, International Champion Laund Lukeo taking the Dog Challenge Certificate and Laund Lucia taking the Bitch Challenge Certificate. These, of course, were the Rough Classes. The Smooth Challenge Certificates were won by Champion Fellman and Laund Latha. On the same day Lukeo and

Lucia won a large Any Variety Brace Class, and with it the cup for the Best Brace in Show. Lukeo also gained the cup for the Best Non-Sporting Dog or Bitch in the show and also Best Non-Sporting Other Than Toy. I do not think that this record has since been equalled, and it was surely one of the happiest days of my father's life.

Lukeo was born in April 1923 (by International Champion Laund Luke ex Laund Lauzan); his brother Laund Leno also became an International Champion.

In comparison with the happy day at Birmingham National, what a sad time it must have been for my father when two more dogs, perhaps even better than the aforementioned, came to a very untimely end along with several more. These heads were considered too good to be allowed to pass into oblivion without some tangible evidence of their merits being kept and many people will have seen the wonderful work that the taxidermist did with the heads of these unfortunate dogs, when visiting the Kennels.

The prefix 'Laund' came from the house in which my parents lived in Rawtenstall, where I was born. It was an ideal place for Collies since there was plenty of ground for kennels and for exercising the dogs. Attached was a small farm, on which my parents kept cattle, hens, and so on, and hence the dogs were never short of fresh eggs and milk. Exercise was always something in which the Laund Wizard believed most strongly and even though the dogs had many acres in which they could gallop, one man spent most of his time taking packs of dogs out for road exercise. These dogs were also taken into the town, where they met people and thus became used to traffic noises.

Coats were something that the Laund Collies were renowned for, and many people thought there was some deep dark secret. This was quite wrong. The only secret was that my father *bred* for coat, and having *got* the coat, made quite sure that these coats were always kept clean and well groomed; no matter how many dogs were housed at Laund, the coats had to be taken care of. This particular chore was usually undertaken by Mary, who was for seventeen years the kennel maid, completely devoted to the dogs. She was at Laund when I was born, and when my mother died in 1957, the first person to be found on the door step was none other than Mary. Mary was not only a kennel maid but also a trusted friend of the family. I do not think that she would ever have left, had she not married and raised a family. Mary was not the only kennel maid we had, but it was Mary who saw to the grooming and kept all the pedigrees and records up to date.

At the age of seven, I handled my first dog in the ring and was a very, very proud little girl on this occasion, winning a second prize. When I was twelve, I was preparing dogs for shows. I have delighted in this task ever since. All these years after, I still get a thrill out of seeing what I think is a well-prepared Collie going to a show.

My greatest ambition as a child was to be able to handle the dogs with the same easy approach as my father. I do not remember ever seeing him with a dog that did not show. He had a happy knack of getting the best out of every single dog. Even though it was not he who saw to their daily routine, they all knew and loved him. Whilst the dogs always looked impeccable when in the ring, father too was very careful about his appearance and would never enter the ring with shoes covered with whitening or anything of that nature as one does sometimes see today.

Living for the dogs as he did, he made three trips to America, to the Westminster Show, on one occasion taking with him the dog who eventually won Best in Show at Madison Square Gardens, the only time this has been won by a Collie.

For my own part, I was quite content to string along with the family kennel, but eventually I bred my first Champion in 1947, Ch. Delwood Betty (by Laund Limitless ex Delwood Susie), thus combining the two kennels owned by the people in Collies who were most dear to me. I do not think I have known two people who thought more of their dogs and their happiness than Col. and Mrs Wilberforce; a visit to Delwood Croft was always a visit I enjoyed to the full.

As time went by, we left Laund House, Rawtenstall and moved to Tarlton where the Launds continued to go from strength to strength. There I grew up, and took over where Mary left off, until I in turn married and left home.

Like everyone else, during the war years we had to curtail breeding. The Government asked people to reduce stock to an absolute minimum. This request was scarcely necessary, as food was most difficult to obtain in any case, and in consequence it was almost impossible to carry on even if one wished.

After the war years, my father again started to breed Collies, but it was uphill work all the way, to get back to the pre-war standard. Eventually he purchased, from Miss de Belle Ball, Ebony of Killartry, who became the kennel's first post-war Champion.

Being left with an invalid mother, my dog breeding actvities were somewhat restricted. It is really only during the last few years that it has been possible for me to continue to breed Collies, albeit on a much smaller scale. I can, however, now manage to get around to the shows as I have longed to do. Since my mother was not really dog-minded, but put up uncomplainingly, for so many years, with a husband and a daughter who thought of little else, the least I could do was to repay her patience and good nature by caring for her in the evening of her life.

I think to breed one's own Champions is much more satisfying than just to buy dogs and to make them Champions. There is tremendous satisfaction to be gained from breeding, rearing and showing a new puppy and this is something which has to be experienced to be realised. Almost as satisfying is to see other people achieving the same ends from stock you have sold to them, particularly if the person concerned happens to be a novice exhibitor.

Throughout the years I have learnt that the dog fraternity, as a whole, are the kindest people one could ever imagine, always ready to lend a helping hand to those in need. One occasionally hears people say that the dog game lies in the hands of the big breeders and the novice never stands a chance. This I do not believe. It is very often just that the so-called novice does not take the pains to prepare or handle his dog to the best advantage, and is very often unwilling to learn. Hence their disappointment when they do not achieve any success. I do not think that any of the real fanciers would ever refuse to help the novice if requested; I think the reverse is true.

In the same way, I do not think that any reliable breeders who care about their Collie stock would export dogs who were not worthy of upholding the tradition of the Collie in this country. I know from personal experience that Collies have gone from Laund to every corner of the world, and in more recent years from many other kennels. Each one of these kennels is more than anxious to supply the very best that they possibly can to the clients overseas who are, in quite a lot of cases, unable to see the dogs before purchasing them. Stock from many of our most well-known kennels has been exported and is responsible for producing dogs of the highest quality, for their new owners.

Left: Champion Laund Peterblue Zöe (born 10 September 1961). Breeders Mrs K. Alexander and Miss E. Dundas-Mouat. By Ch. Hughley Hush Puppy Blue ex Peterblue Martie. Owner Mrs A. L. Bishop.

Right: Champion Laund Luscombe (born 22 August 1967). Breeder and owner Mrs A. L. Bishop. By Ch. Royal Ace of Rokeby ex Ch. Laund Livia.

Writing in Britain, I cannot stress too strongly the need to export only the very, very highest standard of Collies. Great Britain is the mother of the Collie, and residents of this country must try to help our friends in other countries to improve their Collie stock.

With the modern forms of transport now readily available many of the overseas Collie breeders are able to attend our big shows, Cruft's being the one most favoured. It is a common sight to see people from France, Germany, Switzerland, Holland, Norway, Sweden and many

Champion Laund Lucigard (born 8 June 1970). Breeders Mr and Mrs S. Ainscow. By Champion Jefsfire High Regard ex Laund Luciano. Owner Mrs A. L. Bishop.

other countries, all discussing, some in their native language and others in English, the Collies in the ring.

In concluding this chapter I would like to mention that I still have Champion Collies. Most recently, Ch. Laund Lucigard gave me the biggest thrill, winning his first Certificate at the age of 9½ months and his title one day after his first birthday. Since the age restriction for the title was introduced, that must be the quickest possible way of becoming a Champion.

I try hard to maintain the very high standard to which I have always been accustomed and which was originally started more than sixty years ago by my father. We have had Champions of many other breeds, but find that we have always come back to our wonderful friend the Collie.

At this point I would – I don't think it too ridiculous – like to thank the Collies for the many happy years I have spent amongst them, and for the wonderful friends I have made through them.

Finally, may I say sincerely that it was never my intention, when first writing this book, to add this last chapter. So many kind people have requested the story of the Launds, W. W. Stansfield, and myself, so I have answered these requests. I feel sure I may be forgiven, for had it not been for my father and his Launds, I would never have known the Collie.

Appendix 1

Collie Clubs of Great Britain

The names given are those of the Honorary Secretaries.

Ayrshire Collie Club. Mrs E. Mackay, 45 Henderson Avenue, Cambuslang, Scotland.

British Collie Club. Mr A. T. Green, Moss Nook, Wybunbury, Nantwich, Cheshire.

Collie Association. Mrs A. Speding, Brook Cottage, Ripley, Christchurch, Dorset.

Collie Club of Wales. Mrs P. E. Green, Llechau Farm, Llan Harry, Pontyclun, Mid Glamorgan CF7 9JP.

East Anglian Collie Association. Mrs P. M. Barnard, 'Washbay Collies', Watering Lane, West Winch, King's Lynn, Norfolk.

Irish Collie Club. Mr R. Gow, 644 Oldpark Road, Belfast BT14 6QL.

Lancashire and Cheshire Collie Club. Mr W. P. Turner, 32 Chorley Road, Hilldale, Parbold, Nr Wigan.

London and Provincial Collie Club. Mrs L. Westby, 'Sunnyside', Toot Hill, Nr Ongar, Esssex.

London Collie Club. Mrs M. J. P. Punter, 145 White Hill, Chesham, Bucks.

Midland Collie Club. Mrs C. Kinnersley, 14 Church Road, Lilleshall, Nr Newport, Shropshire.

Northumberland and Durham Collie Club. Mr P. Mather, 10 Bickford Terrace, Aycliffe Village, Darlington.

Scottish Collie Club. Mrs E. Sillars, Rowallandale Kennels, Glasgow Road, Eaglesham, Glasgow.

Smooth Collie Club of Great Britain. Mrs I. M. Bratley, 44 Honeyholes Lane, Dunholme, Lincoln LN2 3SQ.

West of England Collie Club. Mrs T. Taylor, Weydown Farm, Lindford, Bordon, Hants.

Yorkshire Collie Club. Mrs L. North, Sewage Farm House, Tankersley, Nr Barnsley, South Yorkshire.

Appendix 2

It is interesting to note that in 1907 there were only fourteen Collie Clubs throughout the world, whilst in 1915, as you will see from the list of Breed Clubs shown, there were twenty-three. Now we have in this country alone, fourteen clubs for Rough Collies, one club for Smooth Collies and three clubs for Bearded Collies, whilst most other dog-loving countries have only one club for the breed. America, with many clubs, is the exception to this rule; no doubt this is due to the vastness of the country.

I believe that in some European countries, some members of the clubs are elected to give an advisory service, study pedigrees and, if called upon, advise the members on the use of stud dogs, and generally assist beginners wishing to purchase their first Collie. I understand that these persons are elected by the committees of the clubs concerned.

COLLIE CLUBS OF THE WORLD IN 1915

Name of Club	Secretary	Area	Annual Subscription	Objects
The Collie Club	J. H. Jacques, Niton, Loughton, Essex	The World	10s. 6d.	Founded 1881. Valuable specials are offered at Shows held in all parts of the United Kingdom. Information from the Hon. Sec. Many Valuable Club Trophies
The Northern Collie Club	T. P. Wood, Charlestown Road, Blackley, Manchester	The Northern & Midland Counties of England and Wales	10s. 6d.	Caters for breeders and others residing in the area named. Valuable special prizes are offered at many Shows. Many Valuable Club Trophies
The Scottish Collie Club	J. Logan Newton Mearns, N.B.	The World	10s. 6d.	Specials offered at various shows. List of Club Judges
Ayrshire Collie Club	T. Jamieson, Rylands, Prestwick, Ayr, N.B.	Confined to Ayrshire	5s. 0d.	
The Smooth Collie Club	W. Baskerville, 19 Delaunays Rd, Crumpsall, Manchester	The United Kingdom	10s. 6d.	Grant Specials at various Shows, but only when a member of the Club Officiates as Judge. Various Club Trophies
Birmingham & Midland Counties Collie Club	E. C. Davis, 64 Shireland Rd, Smethwick, Birmingham	50 miles radius measured from Stephenson Place, Birmingham	5s. 0d.	Open to novice and other fanciers residing in the district named. Two Members Shows and Two Produce Stakes each year. Numerous Club Trophies
The London & Provincial Collie Club	F. W. Western, Sandy, Beds	75 miles N.E. and W. of London and all the Southern Counties of England	7s. 6d.	Supports Shows in South of England with Specials etc. Headquarters: Victoria Hotel, Charterhouse Street E.C. Numerous Club Trophies

Name of Club	Secretary	Area	Annual Subscription	Objects
The Northumberland & Durham Collie Club	H. Walton, 182 Dilston Road, Newcastle-on-Tyne	The Counties of Northumberland & Durham	5s. 0d.	Six Silver Trophies
The Rough Coated Blue Merle Collie Club	A. C. Thompson, 52 Sycamore Rd, Smethwick, Birmingham	The World	10s. 6d.	Guarantees Classes and offers specials at various Shows. Breeders' Trophies, etc.
The Irish Collie Club	Alexander Dalzell, 15 Royal Avenue, Belfast	The whole of Ireland	10s. 6d.	Offer Specials for Competition at various Shows throughout Ireland. Numerous Club Trophies
Collie Club Français	M. Paul Bert, 28 Rue des Mathurins, Paris	France		
The Society of Collie Friends	A. Marx, 32 Goethest, Frankfurt am Main, Germany	The Continent		
The Collie Club of America	J. H. Blackwood, 4 Southard St, Trenton, N.J.	The World	5 dollars	Many Valuable Club Trophies. Produce & Stud Dog Stakes etc.
Dominion Collie Club	Phil. Walker, 254 Magnus Ave., Winnipeg, Man., Canada	Canada		
Pittsburg Collie Club	E. G. Kelty, 416 Noble St, Pittsburg, Pa., U.S.A.	Pittsburgh		
Chicago Collie Club	W. T. Fenton, 4935 Washington Av., Chicago, Ill., U.S.A.	America	5 dollars	
The New England Collie Club	T. B. Middlebrook, 60 N. Market St, Boston, Mass., U.S.A.	New England		Breeders Trophy
The Interstate Collie Club of Philadelphia	D. S. Tinsman, Williamsport, Pa., U.S.A.		3 dollars	

Name of Club	Secretary	Area	Annual Subscription	Objects
Eastern Collie Breeders' Association	J. L. Card, P.O. Box 56, Wellesley, Mass., U.S.A.	Eastern and New England States of America		
St. Louis Collie Club	G. H. Sudhoff, 4266 Arsenal St, St Louis, Mo., U.S.A.			
The New Zealand Collie Club	J. Rennie, Napier, New Zealand	Australasia	5s. 0d.	Trophies: Grand Silver and Gold Challenge Star, value 50 guineas, Solid Silver Collar, Solid Gold Medal
South Australian Collie Club	A. H. Chapman, 125 Grenfell St, Adelaide	South Australia		The President's Cup The Alexander Cup The Breeder's Cup
Victorian Collie Club	Mr. J. McGrath, 416 Queen's Pde, Melbourne, Vic., Australia		5s. 0d.	

Appendix 3

Winners of the Collie Club Challenge Trophy, 1886–1913

Year	Show	
Year	*Show*	
1886	2nd Collie Club	A. H. Megson's Ch. Rutland
1887	28th Kennel Club	S. Boddington's Metchley Wonder
1887	Warwick	J. & W. H. Charles's The Squire
1887	29th Kennel Club	G. R. Krehl's Ch. Eclipse
1888	30th Kennel Club	J. & W. H. Charles's The Squire
1888	3rd Collie Club	J. & W. H. Charles's The Squire
1888	Warwick	J. & W. H. Charles's The Squire
1888	31st Kennel Club	W. P. Arkwright's Blue Ruin
1889	32nd Kennel Club	A. H. Megson's Ch. Metchley Wonder
1889	4th Collie Club	H. C. White's Maney Trefoil
1889	33rd Kennel Club	C. H. Wheeler's Edgbaston Fox
1890	5th Collie Club	J. Bissell's Ch. Charlemagne
1890	Manchester	A. H. Megson's Ch. Metchley Wonder
1890	34th Kennel Club	Capt. Heaton's Ormskirk Dolly
1890	Crystal Palace	A. H. Megson's Ch. Metchley Wonder
1891	35th Kennel Club	Capt. Heaton's Ormskirk Dolly
1891	6th Collie Club	A. H. Megson's Ch. Metchley Wonder
1891	Crystal Palace	T. H. Stretch's Ormskirk Amazement
1892	Liverpool	T. P. Brearley's Portington Beauty
1892	7th Collie Club	A. H. Megson's Ch. Metchley Wonder
1892	36th Kennel Club	T. H. Stretch's Ormskirk Ormonde
1892	Scottish Kennel Club (Edinburgh)	Morton Campbell's Stracathro Ralph
1893	Manchester	J. S. Diggle's Chorlton Phyllis
1893	8th Collie Club	J. & W. Birch's Sefton Hero
1893	37th Kennel Club	J. S. Diggle's Chorlton Precilla
1894	38th Kennel Club	Holme & Halliday's Rufford Ormonde
1894	9th Collie Club	Holme & Halliday's Rufford Ormonde
1894	39th Kennel Club	F. E. & J. B. Jollye's Newmarket Popgun
1895	Manchester	A. H. Megson's Ch. Southport Pilot
1895	10th Collie Club	W. E. Mason's Ch. Southport Perfection
1895	40th Kennel Club	T. H. Stretch's Ormskirk Wellington
1896	11th Collie Club	A. H. Megson's Ch. Southport Perfection
1896	41st Kennel Club	A. H. Megson's Ch. Southport Perfection
1897	12th Collie Club	A. H. Megson's Ch. Ormskirk Emerald
1897	42nd Kennel Club	A. H. Megson's Ch. Southport Perfection
1898	13th Collie Club	A. H. Megson's Ch. Southport Perfection
1898	43rd Kennel Club	A. H. Megson's Ch. Ormskirk Emerald

1899	14th Collie Club	Revd Hans F. Hamilton's Woodmansterne Tartan
1899	44th Kennel Club	A. H. Megson's Ch. Ormskirk Emerald
1900	15th Collie Club	The Princess de Montglyon's Old Hall Beatrice
1900	45th Kennel Club	W. Mercer's Moreland Verda
1901	16th Collie Club	The Princess de Montglyon's Ch. Barwell Masterpiece
1901	46th Kennel Club	Miss P. M. Deveson Jones's Ch. Moreton Hebe
1902	17th Collie Club	Miss P. M. Deveson Jones's Ch. Babette of Moreton
1902	18th Collie Club	W. T. Horry's Ch. Sapho of Boston
1903	19th Collie Club	R. Tait's Ch. Wishaw Clinker
1903	Liverpool	T. H. Stretch's Ormskirk Enchanter
1903	48th Kennel Club	A. H. Megson's Harwood Piccolo
1904	20th Collie Club	W. T. Horry's Ch. Sapho of Boston
1904	49th Kennel Club	R. Tait's Ch. Wishaw Leader
1905	21st Collie Club	R. Tait's Ch. Wishaw Leader
1905	50th Kennel Club	W. T. Horry's Ch. Sapho of Boston
1906	22nd Collie Club	T. H. Stretch's Ch. Ormskirk Venice
1906	51st Kennel Club	W. E. Mason's Ch. Southport Student
1906	Edinburgh	R. Tait's Ch. Wishaw Leader
1906	Birmingham	W. E. Mason's Ch. Southport Student
1907	23rd Collie Club	W. T. Horry's Princess of Tytton
1907	52nd Kennel Club	R. G. Howson's Ch. Eastwood Eminent
1907	Birmingham	W. E. Mason's Ch. Southport Sample
1908	24th Collie Club	W. E. Mason's Ch. Southport Sample
1908	53rd Kennel Club	W. E. Mason's Ch. Southport Sample
1909	Manchester	W. E. Mason's Ch. Southport Sample
1909	54th Kennel Club	W. T. Horry's Ch. Bayard of Tytton
1910	25th Collie Club	W. E. Mason's Ch. Southport Sample
1910	55th Kennel Club	W. T. Horry's Ch. Bayard of Tytton
1911	26th Collie Club	W. Grimshaw's Parkside Pro Patria
1911	56th Kennel Club	W. T. Horry's Ch. Bayard of Tytton
1912	27th Collie Club	H. Ainscough's Parbold Primrose
1912	57th Kennel Club	R. G. Howson's Ch. Eastwood Extra
1913	28th Collie Club	R. G. Howson's Ch. Eastwood Extra

From this list you will see that many well-known names appear more than once. The main winners are as follows:

15 Mr A. H. Megson
 8 Mr W. E. Mason

7   Mr W. T. Horry
5   Mr T. H. Stretch
4   Messrs J. & W. H. Charles
4   Mr R. Tait
3   Mr R. G. Howson

The outstanding winning dogs amongst these listed winners are:

6   Ch. Metchley Wonder
5   Ch. Southport Sample
5   Ch. Southport Perfection
4   The Squire
3   Ch. Ormskirk Emerald
3   Ch. Sapho of Boston
3   Ch. Wishaw Leader
3   Ch. Bayard of Tytton

The British Collie Club Championship Show is now the only show where this trophy is up for competition, and this trophy is the most coveted of all Collie trophies.

The photograph on page 80 shows this trophy in its present day form: older photographs show the Rough Collie and the Smooth Collie in opposite directions.

Appendix 4

KENNEL CLUB List of Fees (as from 1 October 1979)

	£
For all dogs born prior to 1 April 1976	3.00
For dogs born on or after 1 April 1976	
Litter Recording:	
If no dogs in litter registered at the time of recording litter	4.60
If one or more dogs in litter registered at time of recording litter	No fee
Registration in Active Register	4.60
Registration in Obedience Record	4.60
Registration Name Unchangeable (additional fee)	2.30
Re-registration	4.60
Transfer (in Basic or Active Register)	4.60
Loan or use of bitch	1.00
Change of name	5.00

Pedigrees – 3 generations	5.00
Pedigrees – 5 generations	7.50
Pedigrees – Export	17.25
List of Wins (entered in Stud Book)	0.50
Registration of Affix	6.00
Affix Maintenance Fee (Annual)	2.00
Holders of Affix may compound for 20 years on the payment of	15.00
Assumed Name	2.00
Registration of Title	5.00
Maintenance of Title	5.00
Formation of a Branch by a Registered Society	3.00
Maintenance of Title of a Branch of a Registered Society	3.00
Registration of Title of Dog Training Club	5.00
Maintenance of Title of Dog Training Club	5.00
For Shows held under Kennel Club Show Rules:	
Licence to hold a General and Group Championship Show	20.00
Licence to hold a Championship Show	10.00
Licence to hold an Open Show	5.00
Licence to hold a Limited or Sanction Show	2.50
The following Extra Fees are payable for Championship and Open Shows:	
For each 500 exhibits (or part)	2.00
For permission to hold Matches under Kennel Club Regulations	1.00
For permission to hold an Exemption Show	2.50
For permission to hold a Championship Obedience Show as a Separate Event or part of Licence Show	10.00
For permission to hold an Open Obedience Show as a Separate Event or part of a Licence Show	5.00
For permission to hold a Limited or Sanction Obedience Show as a Separate Event or part of a Licence or Sanction Show	2.50
For Working Trials held under Kennel Club Rules:	
Championship Working Trials	10.00
Open Working Trials	5.00
Members' Working Trials	2.50
For Field Trials held under Kennel Club Rules:	
Two-day Meeting	5.00
One-day Meeting	3.00

VAT: All above fees are inclusive of Value Added Tax

Index